ADELAIDE
1445

D0471579

DIFF. ED. ~~20.25~~

IR ~~19.95~~

995
‒
2
4.0

African Mythology

African Mythology

Geoffrey Parrinder

PAUL HAMLYN · LONDON

Contents

THE HAMLYN PUBLISHING GROUP LTD
London New York Sydney Toronto
Astronaut House Feltham Middlesex

Copyright © 1967 Geoffrey Parrinder
All rights reserved
Fourth impression 1975
ISBN 0 600 00042 7
Manufactured in the United States of America

Colour Plates

Uniform with this edition:

Greek Mythology
Egyptian Mythology
North American Indian Mythology
Indian Mythology
Mexican and Central American Mythology
Oceanic Mythology

Introduction

New and old Africa

'There is always something new from Africa', said the Roman writer Pliny. The emergence of many African nation states in the last few years brings news of this continent frequently to the front pages of the newspapers. But there are also many old things in Africa, and some of the oldest forms of human life have recently been discovered in the Great Rift Valley in East Africa. There are still races of Pygmies and Bushmen surviving from ancient times. And behind modern political doctrines there are countless myths and stories which form part of the background to the thinking of African peoples.

Africa is a vast continent, but it divides naturally into two major parts. North Africa, from Egypt to Morocco, and down the river Nile to Ethiopia, belongs mostly to the Mediterranean world, and its dominant religions are Islam and Christianity, with their own thought and story. The Sahara desert and the tropical forests formed an almost impenetrable barrier to knowledge by Europe of the rest of Africa, until the Portuguese braved the seas and rounded the Cape of Good Hope at the end of the fifteenth century.

Africa south of the Sahara is what Arab geographers called Bilad-as-Sudan, the Land of the Black People. That is what it is from the east and west Sudan, through the tropical and equatorial regions, right down into South Africa. Here black people form the overwhelming majority of all the population. It is their mythology that is now to be described.

The Races of Africa

'Black' is a relative term and there is no such thing as a coal black person, any more than there exists a fully white person. There is great variety of shades of colour, height, shape, face and body characteristics, and Africans themselves distinguish between light and dark skinned people in their own communities. The Negro (black) person is roughly described by dark skin, woolly hair, and broad nose. Most Africans are negroes. The name Bantu is often given to the negroes of East and South Africa, but it refers to their languages and not to their race.

Small groups of African peoples distinguishable from the great mass of negroes are Bushmen, Pygmies and Hamites. The Bushmen, including Hottentots, are short in height but not pygmy, with yellowish-brown skin. They travelled down Africa many centuries ago, leaving traces in rock-paintings, and were at the Cape when the first Europeans arrived. Now only about fifty thousand of them remain, mostly living by hunting and rearing cattle.

The Pygmies or Negritos of the river Congo forest regions are very short, between 52 to 58 inches, with broad heads and noses, and they probably come from an early racial type distinct from the negroes. The Hamites are generally light-skinned, though often mixed with negro blood, and are related to Europeans. They are found in North Africa

Right: the bronze panels from Benin, Nigeria, are notable for their characteristic style. Here a royal figure, with coral crown and necklet, bears a two-edged ceremonial sword, flanked by warriors and small attendants carrying musical instruments.

A wooden figure with two horns representing, to the Ibo of Nigeria, fortune and a man's physical strength. Called Ikenga, it symbolizes success in trade, hunting and farming. It is also the personal shrine of a man's 'right hand', or life force. Horniman Museum.

demonstrated by the countless death masks, and by societies which represent the living ancestors. The gods, powers of heaven and earth, and the ancestors, are all 'clouds of witnesses' which form the audience to man's career on earth, and the providence that helps him in trouble.

There is great diversity in African art, for there are innumerable racial groups and languages. One survey counted over two thousand languages and dialects in West Africa alone. But there are two extreme points of view to be avoided. One extreme thinks of all African art as the same, whether in east or west, north or south. The other extreme thinks it is all different, composed of fragments, where each tribe is a separate universe. It is true that there was much division in the past, but there were also great negro empires, mixture of peoples, and racial migrations. Mythology shows that there are often striking similarities between far separated people. But the diversity of art and myth will be met by illustrations from different countries.

Forms of Art

One of the oldest and most widespread forms of African art is painting and engraving on the walls of cave shelters and rocks. These are found in the Sahara, Sudan, East and South Africa, more in the dry than the tropical regions. Many of the East and South African paintings were the work of Bushmen in the past. They are naturalistic, coloured, depicting cattle, wild animals, human beings, and religious figures. Some of these are hundreds, some thousands, of years old, but they are no longer made by Bushmen and so they are not of great value for interpreting mythology narrated today.

Sculpture in the round, in stone, metal or wood, has been practised for a long time in Africa and is still very much alive. It is limited in extent, however, and is found chiefly in West Africa and west Central Africa. This is perhaps partly because the peoples of the Niger-Congo regions have been settled agriculturalists for centuries, whereas the tribes of the east have been nomads or herdsmen.

The oldest tropical African sculptures are of the Nok culture, found in 1943 in northern Nigeria, and at least two thousand years old. They are made of baked clay, terracotta, and are mostly of human heads, either natural in style or lengthened. Since the people who made them are unknown, so are their myths and religion. But they can be compared with naturalistic terracottas and bronzes that were made over a thousand years later some hundreds of miles farther south in Nigeria. The Ifé bronzes, and related Benin bronzes, gave illustrations of human and royal activities.

There is not a great deal of stone sculpture in Africa, and it is found chiefly in Sierra Leone, Nigeria and the Congo; and some across in Zimbabwe in Rhodesia. Soft stone was the chief medium, though quartz and granite were also used. Ivory was carved, often with great delicacy. Clay or mud sculpture is still popular, though as it is highly perishable and cannot be exported, it is not so well known as it deserves.

Of all materials for sculpture wood was and remains the favourite. There are innumerable masks, heads, figures, dolls, head-rests, stools, pipes, bowls, pots, drums, gaming boards, divining trays, screens and doors. And decorative art also appears in rings, bangles, necklaces, girdles, anklets, tattooing and fly-whisks. These form an endless treasury in African art, through which the love of life is expressed.

Religion and Philosophy

Like every race of mankind in every age Africans have many religious beliefs. Some of these are philosophical, in that they consider great questions such as the meaning of life, the origins of all things, the purpose and end of life, death and its conquest. These are often the subject of myths, which are philosophy in parables. More narrowly religious life is shown in rituals, dances, sacrifices and songs.

Proverbs and myths express joy in life and human activity. It is a 'world-affirming' philosophy, in which life on earth is thought of as good, despite human suffering, sex is to be enjoyed, and children are the gift of God. The family is not only husband and wife and children, but the extended family of grandparents, brothers, sisters and cousins, in which old people are honoured and cared for. Life and health are the objects of prayers, maintained by good magic and medicine, and threatened by bad magic and witchcraft. It has often been said that the chief value of African thought is power, vital energy, or dynamism. The world is a realm of powers; the most fruitful life has the most power and harmony.

God, the Supreme Being, is the greatest power of all, the strong one, who possesses life and strength in himself, and from whom every creaturely force is derived. Few if any African peoples have been without belief in the supreme Creator, and even where that belief has been influenced by Islam or Christianity the original idea may still be traced.

The powers of the world act on one another and man tries to keep on good terms with them all. They are not all equal, but are seen to be in a hierarchy of forces. The highest is God, who creates all other powers, and strengthens those who call on him. After God come other great powers, like the chiefs in human society. There are spiritual forces attributed to nature or great human beings, and especially the ancestors who founded the race and who are still interested in it.

It has been suggested that African religion can roughly be depicted as a triangle. At the top, head of all powers, is God. On the two sides of the triangle are the next greatest powers, gods and ancestors. At the base are lower forces, with which magic and medicine are concerned. Man is in the middle, and must live in harmony with all the powers that affect his life, family and work. The powers extend into the animal world, for animals have great forces which need to be watched and harnessed if possible. Even supposedly inorganic nature is not dead, but may be the vehicle of power.

A human being is more than body, he has a spiritual element which is the breath of God, sometimes even called God in man. Body and soul are closely interwoven and are often spoken of as if they were one, though it is known that at death the spirit leaves the body. This is not merely the breath, for people distinguish breath, shadow and influence, from a man's own personality. Medicine is given to heal disease, but a spiritual remedy is also needed.

Human morality is behaviour in society, helping or hurting one's neighbour. It is the interaction of forces, but since they are dependent on God so it is God who is the final judge of man's deeds. Man has the power to kill his neighbour, but he has no right to abuse that power, for he is God's man, and responsible to him for all action. The close relationship of man to God, and the mutual effects of spiritual and material will become clear as the myths are read.

In modern times new religions have come into every part of Africa. Islam and Christianity bring new doctrines, morality, history, scripture,

A bronze head in the form of a miniature jug from the Greek culture of Alexandria. Dating from between the third and first centuries B.C., it portrays a remarkably clear representation of a young negress, one of the race of people who lived beyond the great barriers to the south.

and universalism. But much of the old remains, many Africans are still untouched by the new religions, and even the millions who have joined them are still influenced by the old outlook and mythology.

Mythology

In the mythologies of every continent there can be distinguished great myths, and others that are of less importance. Some myths dominate and show the character of the religious outlook, while others are less central, repetitive, and fanciful. All kinds of myths need to be taken into account, for altogether they show the values which the society holds dear.

Most myths tell how something came to exist; man, the world, certain animals, social affairs. The myths make a 'sacred history' of the people. But naturally the creation of the world comes first and this myth influences others that follow. There could be no stories of creation of men or animals if there was not already a world created for them to enjoy. So the central myth, telling the beginnings of the world, shows that history had a beginning. Legendary events that came later show how the world was changed, and in particular the adventures of man, his discovery of sex, the obligation to work, the coming of death.

Myths also tell about supernatural beings, gods and ancestors. The great heroes of the past provided models for human behaviour later. But they show an end as well as a beginning. For although the Supreme Being and other spirits created and lived on earth, they also left it later on or disappeared. Man too begins and ends his life on earth.

Myths are stories, the product of fertile imagination, sometimes simple, often containing profound truths. They are not meant to be taken too literally. If details sometimes appear childish, so often do those of classical Greece or Egypt. But most myths express serious beliefs in 'human being, eternity, and God'. Modern psychologists, like Jung, have seen in myths clues to the deepest hopes and fears of mankind, not to be despised as stories, but studied carefully for their revelation of the depths of human nature.

The mythology given in this book has been taken from many parts of Africa, but obviously in such a huge continent many people must be given small space. Some tribes have not been studied at all for their mythology, or very little and inadequately. Others have been favoured by detailed and careful recording. The material that is available has been studied as widely as possible, and selections have been made from all over the continent in order to give a picture of some of the major themes in the thought of Africa. Much description of African religion relies upon the external observation of students who do not share the beliefs of the people studied. To record the myths themselves helps to reveal the Africans' own thoughts about religion and life and so, with illustrations of art, this begins to provide the basis for a scripture of African religions.

The first and longest part of this book gives what are most properly called myths. That is, stories of supernatural beings and events. Then some traditions of outstanding interest have been selected, from only a few lands, since all peoples have traditions of their origins and rulers, and these are endless. Finally some fables of animal life are included, because these are among the most popular of all African stories. The fables show man living close to the animal and natural worlds, but they also project human feelings on to animals and reveal attitudes and actions of men which are both praised and blamed.

Model of the universe in the mythology of the Dogon of Mali. The circular base is the sun and the square top the sky, with a circle for the moon. It is called the Granary of the Master of Pure Earth. The first ancestor came down from the sky by the steps at the side to mark out land for fields for his descendants. From Griaule: *Conversations with Ogotemmêli*.

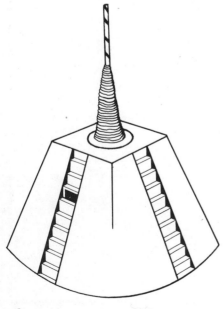

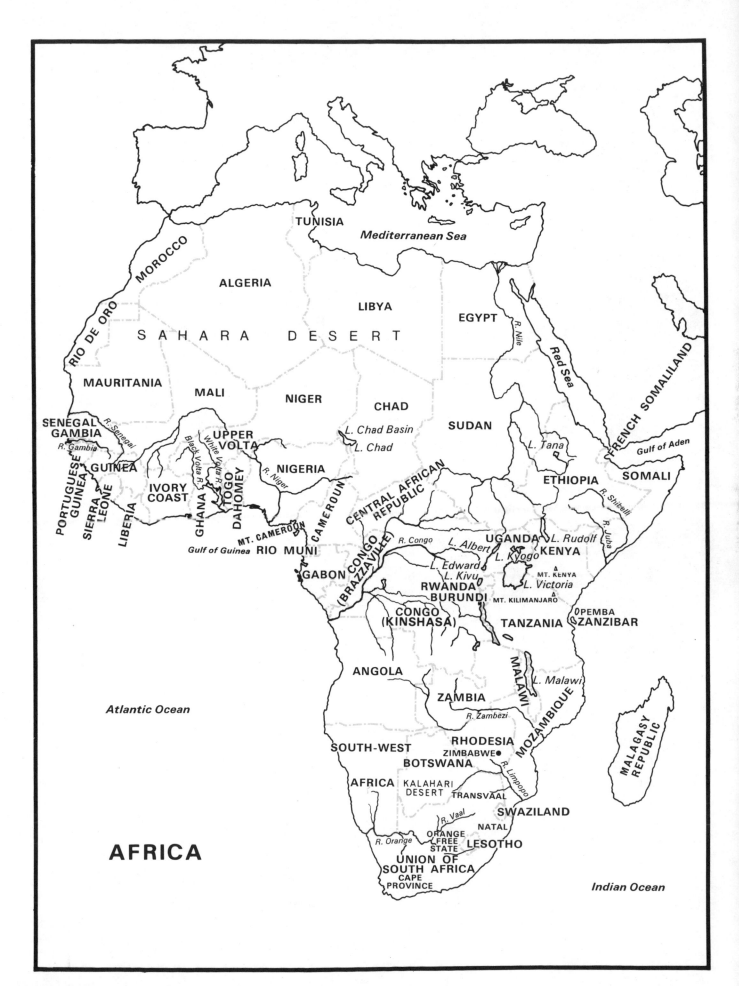

AFRICA

MOROCCO
RIO DE ORO
ALGERIA
TUNISIA
Mediterranean Sea
LIBYA
EGYPT
R. Nile
Red Sea
S A H A R A   D E S E R T
MAURITANIA
MALI
NIGER
CHAD
SUDAN
FRENCH SOMALILAND
Gulf of Aden
SENEGAL
GAMBIA
R. Senegal
R. Gambia
UPPER VOLTA
L. Chad Basin
L. Chad
L. Tana
ETHIOPIA
SOMALI
GUINEA
PORTUGUESE GUINEA
SIERRA LEONE
LIBERIA
IVORY COAST
Black Volta R.
White Volta R.
GHANA
TOGO
DAHOMEY
NIGERIA
R. Niger
CAMEROUN
CENTRAL AFRICAN REPUBLIC
R. Shibelli
R. Juba
MT. CAMEROON
Gulf of Guinea
RIO MUNI
GABON
CONGO (BRAZZAVILLE)
R. Congo
L. Albert
UGANDA
L. Rudolf
KENYA
L. Edward
L. Kivu
L. Kyogo
MT. KENYA
L. Victoria
RWANDA
BURUNDI
MT. KILIMANJARO
CONGO (KINSHASA)
TANZANIA
PEMBA
ZANZIBAR
ANGOLA
MALAWI
L. Malawi
ZAMBIA
R. Zambezi
MOZAMBIQUE
Atlantic Ocean
MALAGASY REPUBLIC
SOUTH-WEST AFRICA
RHODESIA
ZIMBABWE•
BOTSWANA
KALAHARI DESERT
R. Limpopo
TRANSVAAL
SWAZILAND
R. Vaal
NATAL
ORANGE FREE STATE
LESOTHO
R. Orange
UNION OF SOUTH AFRICA
CAPE PROVINCE
Indian Ocean

17

The Creator

There is no doubt that nearly all, if not all, African peoples believe in a Supreme Being, the creator of all things. A supreme god is named in the earliest dictionary of a Bantu language, compiled in 1650, and in Bosman's description of West Africa published in 1705. Belief in a Supreme Being is a thoroughly negro African conception, current long before there were any established Christian or Moslem missions in the interior regions of tropical or southern Africa.

The names of the Supreme Being vary a great deal, of course, due to the many different languages of Africa. But there are some names which are common over wide areas. The name Mulungu for God is used in East Africa and has been adopted in about thirty translations of the Bible. In central Africa the name Leza is used by a number of different peoples. And in the western tropics, from Botswana to the Congo, variants of the name Nyambe are found. It is possible that the name Nyame for God in Ghana is related to Nyambe, but West African peoples have many other names: Ngewo, Mawu, Amma, Olorun, Chukwu, and so on to denote the Supreme Being. In this book the English word God will sometimes be used, as the nearest equivalent of an African conception of the Supreme Being.

God is the Creator, and myths told about him seek to explain the origins of the world and man. He is transcendent, living in heaven, to which men naturally look up and recognize his greatness. It is often thought that he used to dwell on earth, but he retired to the sky, usually because of some human misdeed.

Although he is the greatest of all, there are lesser spirits which are often prominent in religious worship. Gods of storm, earth, forest, water, and the like, are popular. In West Africa there are many temples for such deities, though in other parts of the continent they may be only vaguely reverenced and there are relatively few temples for their worship. But the spirits of the dead are important everywhere. Belief in life after death, perhaps the most ancient and tenacious religious belief of all mankind, is found everywhere in Africa. The many secret societies, masked dancers, and ancestral rituals prove this.

It is strange that there are very few temples of the supreme God, while lesser deities and ancestors have many holy places for their worship. This has led some people to think that he is a distant deity, a necessary Creator but now an absentee, often forgotten or only rarely invoked. But the myths to be recorded later will show that he is not only a past Creator, but appears very often in the ordinary events of human life. Wise old Africans, when questioned on this point of the absence of worship, say that God is too great to be contained in a house. Solomon in his wisdom said much the same.

Although in myths the Supreme Being is spoken of in a personal manner, as if he were a man with a body, and often with a wife and family, yet many African sayings and proverbs speak of God in an abstract and philosophical fashion. God is the abstract idea, the cause. He is also a personal deity, generally benevolent, who cares for men and does not strike them with terror. Further, he is often an indwelling power, which

A dance mask in carved wood. In spite of the weight—this one is over four feet high—they were carried on the head by dancers at Yoruba festivals. British Museum.

sustains and animates all things. God knows everything, he sees all, he can do whatever he wishes. He is justice, rewarding the good and punishing the wicked. He is the final court of appeal, to which even the poorest and most insignificant can go, when they get no redress from other gods and chiefs. Although men speak of him with a face, and hands and legs, as does the Bible, yet in reality God has no form. He cannot be contained in a temple, the thunder is his voice, yet he is greater than the storm. He is indescribable, the only reality.

These divine attributes appear in proverbs and myths, but of course in stories more tangible human characteristics appear. As Creator he made all things and fixed the customs of every people. He laid out the countryside, arranged the mountains in their places, put in rivers, planted trees and grass. He even fixed the ant-hills that rise up red and hard, great cones made by the termite white ant.

As Moulder of All he shaped things, like a woman fashioning pots that she makes out of clay. He put things together and constructed them, like a builder making a house of dried clay, layer by layer.

God is father and mother of men and animals. He is not often thought of as having been born, since he is eternal, but there is a story that says he was born of a woman with one breast. His wife is spoken of, and the hard brown rings which form the body of a centipede or millipede are called 'the ivory bracelets of the wife of God'. Yet some peoples think of him as possessing dual natures, male and female, and a famous writer in Ghana used to speak of 'Father-Mother God'. Of course God is beyond sex, though in story he usually appears in human form.

The Supreme Being is in heaven and so he is particularly concerned with rain, upon which men depend entirely for their life. He is rarely associated with the sun, for in the tropics the sun is always present, and there is no need of chants and sacrifices to bring the sun back again, as in ancient Europe and Japan. God rends the sky with lightning and moves the forest so that the trees murmur. Instead of saying 'it', as we do when we say 'it is hot', Africans often say 'God is fiercely hot', 'God is falling as rain', 'God makes the drumming of thunder'. To say 'God is burying eggs' means that as a crocodile hides eggs in the sand and comes back later without mistake, so the thunder will return in time. When rain begins the pleasant freshness is described by saying that 'God has softened the day'. The rainbow is often called 'the bow of God', who is like a hunter.

God is high and over all things, he 'covers' us like the sky. He is powerful and wise, but not easy to understand. There are mysteries about God, he is 'the incomprehensible being'. This comes from the nature of life itself, which has sorrow as well as joy. Like an almighty Fate, he is held responsible for evil and suffering. A man who has lost all his children through sickness or accident may be called 'one on whom God has looked'. There are moving myths of men and women who went to God to find out the reason for their sufferings.

Some of the names given to God in African ritual, proverbs and myths, show what men think of his character and attributes. He is first of all Creator, Moulder, Giver of Breath and Souls, God of Destiny. His work in nature is shown by titles such as Giver of Rain and Sunshine, One who Brings the Seasons, the One who Thunders, the Bow in the Sky, the Fire-lighter. The divine greatness is indicated by the names Ancient of Days, the Limitless, the First, the One who Bends Even Kings, He who Gives and Rots, the One who Exists of Himself, the One you Meet Everywhere.

Ivory carving is much practised in tropical Africa. This fine example from Benin, Nigeria, may be a goddess or a simple symbol of fertility. Sculptures of African womanhood emphasize the mystery and power of life in the firmly moulded body and the calm, accepting face.

The providence of God is shown by names such as Father of Babies, Great Mother, Greatest of Friends, the Kindly One, God of Pity and Comfort, the Providence who Watches All Like the Sun, the One on whom Men Lean and Do Not Fall. Finally there are mysterious and enigmatic titles: the Great Ocean Whose Headdress is the Horizon, the Great Pool Contemporary of Everything, the One Beyond All Thanks, the Inexplicable, the Angry One, the Great Spider – the clever insect who comes into many stories.

Creating the Earth

The primal myth occurs in many forms, and specimens will now be given from different countries. Shorter references to creating the earth will also be found in stories about the creation of men and traditions of the first ancestors.

The Yoruba of Nigeria say that in the beginning the world was all marshy and watery, a waste place. Above it was the sky where Ol-orun, the Owner of the Sky, lived with other divinities. The gods came down sometimes to play in the marshy waste, coming down spider's webs which hung across great gaps like fairy bridges. But there were no men yet, for there was no solid ground. One day Ol-orun – Supreme Being – called the chief of the divinities, Great God (Orisha Nla) into his presence. He told him that he wanted to create firm ground and asked him to set about the task (in some versions it was the Oracle god who did the work, see page 88). Great God was given a snail shell in which there was some loose earth, a pigeon and a hen with five toes. He came down to the marsh and threw the earth from the snail shell into a small space. Then he put the pigeon and the hen on the earth, and they started to scratch and scatter it about. Before long they had covered much of the marsh and solid ground was formed.

When Great God went back to report to the Supreme Being the latter sent a Chameleon to inspect the work. The Chameleon is a prominent figure in many African myths, and it is noted for its slow careful walk, its change of colour to suit its environment, and its big rolling eyes. After a first inspection the Chameleon reported that the earth was wide but not dry enough. Then he was sent again, and this time he said it was both wide and dry. The place where creation began was called Ifé, meaning 'wide', and later the word Ilé, 'house', was added, to show that it was the house from which all other earthly dwellings have originated. Ilé-Ifé has been ever since the most sacred city of the Yoruba people, and this explanatory story is put out to justify its eminence.

The making of the earth took four days, and the fifth was reserved for the worship of Great God, and ever since a week of four days has been observed, each one of which is sacred to a divinity. Then the Supreme Being-Creator sent Great God back to earth to plant trees, to give food and wealth to man. He gave him the palm nut of the original palm tree, whose nuts give oil and whose juice supplies drink. Three other common trees were planted, and later rain fell to water them.

Meanwhile the first men had been created in heaven and were then sent to earth. Part of the work of making men was entrusted to Great God, and he made human beings from the earth and moulded their physical features. But the task of bringing these dummies to life was reserved for the Creator alone. It is said that Great God was envious of this work of giving life, and he decided to spy on the Creator to see how

it was done. So one day when he had finished moulding human forms, he shut himself in with them overnight and hid behind them so that he could watch. But the Creator knew everything and he sent Great God into a deep sleep, and when he woke up the human beings had come to life. Great God still makes only the bodies of men and women, but he leaves distinct marks on them and some bear signs of his displeasure.

Heavenly Twins

Neighbours of the Yoruba are the Fon of Dahomey, and they have different creation stories. They speak of a supreme God (Mawu) and many other beings related to him. But Mawu is sometimes called male and sometimes female; Mawu has a partner called Lisa, and they may be spoken of as twins. One myth says that these twins were born from a primordial mother, Nana Buluku, who created the world and then retired. Mawu was the moon and female, having control of the night and dwelling in the west. Lisa was male, the sun, and lived in the east. They had no children when they first took up their stations, but eventually they came together in an eclipse. Whenever there is an eclipse of the sun or moon it is said that Mawu and Lisa are making love.

The primeval twins, Mawu-Lisa, became parents of all the other gods. These were all twins too, seven pairs. There is difference of opinion as to which were born first and so are seniors, but probably the gods of earth, storm and iron are first in succession. It is said that one day Mawu-Lisa called all their children together, and gave each of them a domain. The first set of twins was entrusted with the rule of Earth and they were told to take whatever they wished from heaven. The twins of Storm were told to stay in the sky and rule over thunder and lightning. Then the Iron twins were told that since they were the strength of their parents they must clear the forests and make cultivable land; they should also give tools and weapons to men. Another pair were ordered to live in the sea and all waters and rule the fishes. Other hunters were sent into the bush to rule over birds and beasts and care for trees. The space between the earth and sky was the domain of other deities who were entrusted with the life-span of human beings and they were told to return from time to time to the Supreme Being (Mawu) to tell of all that happened in the world. These Sky gods also prevented other gods from being seen by men, and so men speak of gods as sky or spirit.

To each of the gods the Creator gave a special language and these are the ritual languages spoken by the priests and mediums of the gods in their songs and oracles. One spirit, a divine messenger (Eshu, Legba, see page 90-91), was given knowledge of all languages and serves today as intermediary between gods and gods, and between men and all the divinities. It will be noticed that the Supreme Being is often called Mawu, without mention of Lisa, and the tendency to unity of thought makes this deity supreme in practice, without mention of male or female nature.

The Universal Calabash

A calabash is a gourd, like a melon or pumpkin, whose hard rind makes it useful to men when the soft inner pulp is cleaned out. It is useful as a waterpot, or with hard seeds in it can be used as a rattle. A round calabash, cut in two horizontally, is put in some temples and contains

From the north of the Congo (Brazzaville) an effigy of an ancestor, made of wood covered with brass. The formal design suggests the awesomeness of the dead; the winged head shows power. The lozenge shape is common in the symbolic art of the peoples of this region. Horniman Museum.

Left: there is little sculpture beyond the Niger and the Congo basins, except in Malagasy where these grave posts of ancestors in simple and expressive form show the continuity of life. A Malagasy myth says that God saw his daughter Earth making clay images, and he blew into them to give them life, but when men and women became too numerous he took their breath away again and death came to the world.

A seated female figure from the Bambara people of Mali. It is believed to have been an ancestor cult figure, of the kind to which special honour was paid in funerary rites.

small offerings or symbolical objects. The calabash is often decorated with carving on upper and lower shells, with a great variety of designs as well as pictures of human beings, animals and reptiles.

In Dahomey the universe is sometimes said to be a sphere like a round calabash, the horizon being where the upper and lower lips of a divided calabash meet. That is where the sky and sea mingle, in an ideal place inaccessible to man. The earth is thought to be flat, floating inside the larger sphere, as a small calabash may float in a big one. Within the sphere are waters, not only at the horizon but under the earth. This is explained by saying that if one digs into the ground water is always discovered and so water must surround the whole earth. The sun, moon and stars move in the upper part of the calabash. The place of the dead is uncertain, some think that they are above the earth, and others that they are in the invisible part below the inhabited earth.

When God created all things his first concern was to gather the earth together, fix the bounds of the waters, and join the calabash close. A divine snake coiled itself round the earth to bring it together and keep it firm. He carried God here and there, establishing order and by his essential movement sustaining all things.

Serpent of Eternity

The snake has had a fascination for men in every land; it is mysterious, fearful and immortal. Because it goes on its belly without feet, living apart from and dangerous to all living beings, it is feared. Because it sheds its skin yet continues to live, it is regarded as immortal. A snake with its tail in its mouth, apparently swallowing itself yet with no beginning or end, like a circle and sphere, is symbolic of eternity. This is seen in art, depicted on cloth patterns, painted on walls, and worked out in metal. But not all snakes are identical, and the favourite is the python which is not poisonous.

When the world was created, say the Fon, the snake gathered the earth together with its coils and gave men a place in which to live. It still sustains the world and its coils must not be loosened lest everything disintegrates. It is said that there are 3,500 snake coils above the earth and 3,500 below. In another version of the story the snake erected four pillars at each of the cardinal points to uphold the heavens, and it twisted itself round the pillars to keep them upright. The three primary colours of black, white and red are the clothes which the snake puts on at night, day and twilight, and these colours are twined round the heavenly pillars.

The snake is essentially motion, the symbol of flowing movement, like reeds in water. It is submerged in waters under the earth, dwelling in the ocean and so representing the greatest power in unceasing movement. The coils of the snake are not still but revolve round the earth and set the heavenly bodies in motion. The snake may still be seen in quiet pools, running rivers, and in the ocean. Or a flash of light may be seen, cleaving the waters, and its voice sounds abroad. In the beginning the snake found only stagnant water on earth, so he traced out courses for the streams and channels for rivers and thus the world received life. When the snake carried the Creator through the length and breadth of the world mountains appeared wherever they stopped.

A further version says that the snake was created first, and it carried the Creator everywhere in its mouth making the world as it is now. Each night when they stopped great mountains of the snake's excrement appeared, and so when men dig into mountains they find treasure. When the Creator had finished he saw that there were too many mountains, trees and large animals for the earth to carry. How could he stop the earth from sinking into the sea that surrounded it? He asked the snake to coil itself up with its tail in its mouth to support the earth. The snake became like the circular carrying pad that people put on their heads to support water pots or other weights. Since the snake does not like heat the sea keeps him cool. God told some red monkeys, who live in the sea, to make iron bars for his food whenever he is hungry. Every so often the snake shifts his position a little and there is an earthquake. If the monkeys fail to feed him with iron the snake will be obliged to eat its own tail. When this happens the earth, weighed down with even more burdens than at the beginning, with more men and houses, will slide into the ocean, and that will be the end of the world.

God, Earth and Spirits

In the western Sudan, south of Timbuctoo and the bend of the river Niger, live the Dogon people. Remarkable ideas of religion and mythology have been collected among them in recent years that are quite distinct in African studies. It is important to include them, but it must be stressed that it is not known how far other people share similar beliefs, and they cannot be taken as typical. These world views were revealed by a blind old man, Ogotemmêli, who had been chosen to declare the secret mythology of the tribe to his European friends.

In the beginning the one God, Amma, created the sun and moon like pots, his first invention. The sun is white hot and surrounded by eight rings of red copper, and the moon is the same shape with rings of white copper. The stars came from pellets of clay that Amma flung into space. To create the earth he squeezed a lump of clay, as he had done for the stars, and threw it into space. There it spread out flat, with the north at the top, and its members branched out in different directions like the body, lying flat with its face upwards.

Amma was lonely and drew near to the female earth to unite himself with it. But his passage was barred by a red termite hill. He cut this down and union took place, but the interference made it defective and instead of twins being born, which would have been natural, a jackal was born instead. This jackal was a trouble to him afterwards. The myth justifies female circumcision, which is practised by the Dogon and many other African peoples.

There was further union between God and the Earth and twins were born. They were like water and green in colour. Their top half was human and the bottom half snake-like. They had red eyes and forked tongues, sinuous arms without joints, and their bodies covered with short green hair, shining like water. They had eight members and were born perfect. These two spirits were called Nummo, and they went up to heaven to get instructions from God, since he was their father and they were made from his essence which is the life-force of the world, from which comes all motion and energy. This force is water and the Nummo are in all water, or seas and rivers and storms, in fact they are water. They are also light and emit it constantly.

When the Nummo spirits looked down from the sky they saw Mother Earth, naked and in disorder. So they came down bringing the bunches

In Sierra Leone and Guinea many ancient soapstone or steatite figures are found which are called 'rice gods', though they may represent ancestors. They are said to have an 'archaic smile' though the sculptors may not have intended this.

23

Terracotta head from Nok, northern Nigeria. The first example was discovered in 1943, and such heads are estimated to be over two thousand years old. They are some of the most naturalistic of tropical African sculptures.

Right: mask of the Mpongwe of Congo (Brazzaville), carved from wood with the face painted white with kaolin. With the impassive features, decorated forehead and elaborate hairstyle it represents a female ancestor.

of fibres from heavenly plants which they made into two bunches to clothe the Earth in front and behind like a woman. The fibres were moist and full of the essence of the Nummo spirits. By means of this clothing the Earth obtained a language, elementary but sufficient for the beginning.

The jackal, deceitful firstborn of God, was jealous of his mother's possession of language. He seized the fibre skirt in which language was embodied. The earth resisted this sinful attack and hid in her own womb, symbolized as an anthill in which she changed into an ant. The jackal pursued her, and although the Earth dug down deep, she was not able to escape. The jackal seized his mother's skirt, gained the power of speech, and so he is able to reveal the plans of the Supreme Being to diviners.

The result of this unfilial attack was the defilement of the Earth, and Amma decided to create live beings without her. But when he had formed their organs the Nummo spirits saw that there was a danger of twin births disappearing. So they drew a male and female outline on the ground, on top of one another. And so it was, and has been ever since, that every human being has two souls at first, man is bi-sexual. But a man's female soul is removed at circumcision, when he becomes a true man; and the corresponding event happens to a woman at excision. The myths continue with the coming of the first men, and though they still refer back to God, they will be considered later under a separate heading. Meanwhile the gifts of God to man occur in a number of myths.

God sends Food

Across the other side of Africa the Ila people of Zambia say that when God sent men to earth long ago he gave them grain for food and charged them to take good care of it. When they got to the land men sowed the grain and there was a great harvest. The corn was gathered, put into bins, and then they all sat down to eat. But men were greedy and ate all through the day, as well as at morning and evening. When they were full they said that since there was so much grain it would never be finished, everybody was satisfied now and the grain could be burnt on the fire. So they set to and burnt all the grain. Then in due course a famine arose and men had no food. They left their village and went to God to say what had come about. God told them they were silly people, eating till they were satiated and then burning the rest. Now he said he would give them fruits, and since they had burnt the grain they would have nothing but roots and fruit to eat. It has been so ever since. Men act in a foolish way. The grain is wasted; some brew beer from it, others burn it, others eat too much, or at the wrong times, or use the grain improvidently. Then when stores are exhausted they have to turn to roots and fruit. The story refers to the hunger that comes when supplies have run low and before the new harvest is ready, and blames this on human greed and improvidence.

A story told in Malagasy of the origin of rice says that a woman took her child to the river one day and let it play there while she was working. The child saw an insect and asked his mother what it was that jumped so high. She replied that it was a grasshopper, and he asked her to catch it for him. So the mother caught it and gave it to the child as a plaything. But when she was ready to go home the child cried because the grasshopper had jumped away. The mother searched everywhere

but could not find it, and the child was so sad that it became ill and died. The mother wept bitterly and her cries went up to God. God took pity on the woman and told her to bury the child in a deep marsh. A month later a plant began to grow from the spot where the child had been buried. It grew up and bore grains, which birds came to eat when they were ripe. Then God told the woman to pound the grains, cook and eat them. This was the beginning of rice, so called after the name of the child.

Another Malagasy story tells of rice and of the work appropriate to every man. There were four men on earth, each with his own work, but they could not agree together. The first was a hunter with a spear, the second a trapper, the third gathered fruit, and the fourth cultivated the soil. As they never agreed they decided to ask God to change their lot, so that they could live together. When they arrived God was pounding rice, and said that he had no time for them that day, but he gave each of them a handful of rice and told them to keep it till he saw them in two or three days time. Then each of the men went his way. The first saw some game, dropped the rice, and went hunting. The second heard a bird screech, put down his rice and went after it, and when he came back the rice was gone. The third reached for some fruit and dropped his rice in a river. The fourth put down his rice and began to dig the ground; when he came back the wind had blown the rice about, but he managed to gather some of it. When God called the men he asked for the rice and each told his story. Then God said that it showed that their fate could not be changed. The hunter remains a hunter, and so on. Thereafter each man stuck to his lot and was content.

God and Fire

The discovery of fire marks a great stage in human life, and there are many stories which agree that at first there was no fire, and it came from God or the celestial regions. A story of the Ila people say that it was brought from heaven by the Mason-wasp. This is one of the commonest insects of Africa, with blue wings, yellow middle and striped legs. It builds mud nests on any object: walls, curtains, sticks and fireplaces; there it lays eggs, puts in grubs to feed them and goes off; in due time the eggs hatch out, break free from the cell, and eventually the new insects lay eggs in the same way, never having met their parents. Because the Mason-wasp likes the fireplace so the stories see him bringing fire from heaven, like the Greek Prometheus. Originally there was no fire on earth, and all the birds and insects came together to ask how they could keep warm. Someone said that perhaps there was fire with God. The Mason-wasp said he would go and see, if somebody would accompany him. So the vulture, fish-eagle and crow volunteered. They said farewell to the birds and flew high in the sky. About ten days later some bones fell down to the ground, they were those of the vulture. Next, more bones fell down, from the fish-eagle. Finally other small bones which were those of the crow. The Mason-wasp went on alone for thirty days, resting on the clouds but never managing to reach the top of the sky. God heard that the Mason-wasp was near and came down to ask where he was going. The Mason-wasp said nowhere in particular, his friends had fallen behind, but he had kept on flying to reach the Chief of All to beg for some fire. God took pity on him, and said that since the Mason-wasp alone had reached him he would be head of all birds and insects in future. He told him to build a house for his child near a fireplace, leave the egg

there, return after many days, and he would find it had changed into a wasp like himself. So it has been ever since. The Mason-wasp builds his nest near the fireplace because God commanded it to do so. There is some confusion in the story between the gift of fire and building the nest, perhaps because two stories are mingled in it.

The Dogon tale of fire says that when the first ancestors of men were ready to come to earth they had no fire. The Nummo spirits, children of God and earth, were heavenly blacksmiths and an ancestor stole a piece of the sun from their smithy. The female Nummo threw a flash of lightning at him, but the ancestor protected himself with a leather bellows that he had made to contain the piece of sun and lightning could not penetrate it. Then the male Nummo cast a thunderbolt, and this also failed, though the ancestor slid down a rainbow to earth with such speed that he broke his arms and legs. Formerly these limbs had been sinuous, like those of the Nummo, but since that time men have had joints at knees and elbows. The story continues with the granary that the ancestor made, and will be told later.

There are several interesting myths of fire told by the Pygmies in the Congo forests. They say that they were the first to obtain fire, and later passed it on to the negroes who think they are their masters. Once when a Pygmy was chasing an elephant he arrived by chance at the village of God and saw fire burning. He seized a brand and ran off with it, but God caught him and made him give it back. Three times this happened, as Pygmy stories often have three stages. Finally God was tired and made a fence of liana round his village. But the Pygmy jumped over the liana easily and brought the fire safely back to his camp.

A variant Pygmy myth says that originally God had fire, in front of which his old mother sat most of her days trying to keep warm. He

Rock painting from the Brandenberg Mountains in South West Africa. The Bushmen were great engravers and painters on rock surfaces in red, black, yellow, white and brown. The subjects are usually hunting, fighting or dancing. The practice of the art has almost completely died out, as there are only a few thousand Bushmen left and the survivors rarely know the meaning of the designs. This is clearly a hunting scene and the central figure is called the White Lady, though no more is known about it than the colour.

27

The Bambara of Mali are unique in carving double antelope headdresses, highly stylized, used in rites which re-enact myths of the birth of agriculture.

also had a swing of lianas on which he flew through the air from one river to another. When God was away on his swing a Pygmy who was lost in the forest came to the place where fire was burning. God's mother was asleep and the Pygmy stole the fire. She awoke with the cold and called her son. God comforted her, jumped on his swing, caught the Pygmy and brought the fire back. The Pygmy told his story to his fellows in their camp and another offered to fetch the fire, but the same misfortune happened to him. Then a third took some feathers off a bird and began to fly. He flew about until he reached the village of God, where he also stole the fire. The mother of God called her son and he chased the Pygmy, but although they jumped over the hills and valleys, up to the sky and down to the depths, the Pygmy escaped, till at last God admitted that he was his equal and brother. But when God arrived back home he found his mother stretched out dead with cold, and then God decreed that henceforth men should die as a punishment. So although men have fire they have death as well.

Another Pygmy story says that originally it was the chimpanzees who possessed fire, and one day a Pygmy found their village and was delighted to sit round the fire. At once he began to plan how to seize it and take it home. One day, wearing a new bark-cloth which hung down to the ground, he came to the village of the chimpanzees. The old chimpanzees were busy in their plantation, and the young ones made fun of the Pygmy in his strange cloth. But they gave him bananas to eat and he sat down so near the fire that his cloth began to smoulder. The young chimpanzees warned him that he was catching fire, but he told them not to worry because the cloth was plenty long enough. He sat even closer to the fire till the cloth caught light, and then he jumped up and ran away as fast as he could. The young chimpanzees were taken aback, and called their elders, who set off in pursuit. But the Pygmy was too far ahead and when the chimpanzees reached his village there were fires everywhere. The chimpanzees reproached the Pygmy for stealing the fire, instead of buying it honestly, and they went home grumbling. In another version it is said that the chimpanzees then abandoned their village, and ever since they have lived in the forest without fire or bananas and only eat wild fruit.

The Coming of Darkness

A story told by the Kono people of Sierra Leone says that when God first made the world it never became really dark or cold. The sun shone during the day and at night the moon gave a twilight in which everything could be seen clearly. But one day God called the Bat and gave him a basket to carry to the Moon. In the basket was darkness, but God did not say what the Moon should do with it, though he promised to come and explain later on. The Bat flew off with the basket on his back and set out for the Moon. But on the way he got tired and put down the basket for a rest, and went off to get food. During his absence some animals found the basket by the wayside and started to open it, thinking there was food in it. Just as they were taking the cover off the Bat came back, but darkness had already escaped. Ever since then the Bat sleeps all day long, but in the twilight and dark he begins to fly about everywhere, trying to catch the dark, put it back in the basket, and take it to the moon according to the command of God. But the Bat never succeeds in catching the darkness, although he chases about in every direction, and before long day returns and the Bat has to sleep again. This kind of story, with its resemblance to the Greek myth of Pandora's box, is very popular in many parts of Africa. As will be seen later, it has parallels in stories of the coming of death.

The Divine Family

God is often credited with a family in heaven, and the Pygmy story of his mother has been told. But generally few details are given and the stories in which this family is mentioned may simply give material for some creaturely behaviour. An Ila story says that the Blue Jay was already married, but custom did not forbid him seeking another wife, even from the highest quarter. Later on a story will be told about a man who would be satisfied with no other marriage than with the daughter of the sun. Here the Blue Jay went to God and asked for the hand of his daughter. God did not refuse, but said that his child must not be given the meat of any large animal to eat. The Blue Jay accepted this condition; he brought the daughter of God to his earthly home, and told his first wife and his mother of the divine law, that his new wife must never eat the flesh of any large animal. His mother agreed but his first wife was jealous. When the Blue Jay next went hunting he killed a zebra and a small duiker deer. He took them home and told his first wife to cook the meat, but not to give the daughter of God any flesh of the zebra. She obeyed, but when the Blue Jay was out again she offered the daughter of God the zebra meat, saying that it was the duiker. God's daughter tasted the meat and fell down dead. When the Blue Jay came in he asked what his new wife had died of, but his first wife replied that she did not know.

So the Blue Jay flew up to heaven to take the news to God. God reproached him for disobeying his command and sent him back to earth. Thirty days later a small cloud arose and God opened his mouth and made thunder. Then he came down and blew open the grave where his daughter was buried and carried her off to the sky. He took the Blue Jay too but did not take him to heaven – halfway there God hurled him down to earth, and all that arrived on the ground were some very small bones. The story is told to explain the weird cry of the Blue Jay when it flies high in the air. This sounds like a cry of death, and mothers distract children's attention from such a cry lest it become an omen of death for them. The feathers of the Blue Jay are used as a charm against sudden death. The story also shows the danger of neglecting divine commands, the jealousy of a rival wife, and the responsibility of the head of a house for whatever happens in his own dwelling.

Suffering and the Supreme Being

God is the creator of the world, the ordainer of human lives, and the final court of appeal when calls upon other gods and ancestors have failed. So there are some moving stories of men and women who have suffered greatly in their lives and try to get an explanation of their woes from the Great Disposer of All.

An Ila story tells of an old woman who had been much troubled in her life. She came from a big family, but God Leza, 'the One who Besets', smote them all. While she was still a child her father and mother died

Pestle and mortar for pounding grain from Dahomey. A famous myth says that at first the sky was low down, but people became too familiar with it, and when a woman hit it in the eye with a long pestle the sky retired in anger to the distance where it has been ever since. Horniman Museum.

Portrait head of an ancestor of the Mende, Sierra Leone. Made of pink soapstone, such heads are often called 'rice gods' when found in fields, but they probably represent early ancestors.

and left her an orphan. As she grew up her relatives perished also. The woman managed to get a husband and bear children, yet in undue season her husband passed away. The woman thought that at least she would be spared the children of her womb, and they lived for a time and bore their own children. But then the One who Besets struck again and both children and grandchildren died, leaving the woman alone as a miserable old crone with nobody to care for her. She thought that at last she would die, and join her family.

But then a strange thing happened. Instead of dying the woman gained energy and became younger. Some people would have attributed this rejuvenation to witchcraft, saying that the woman had eaten her relatives and taken their soul-stuff to strengthen her own. But the woman knew that this was not so, and she determined to put her new powers to a great purpose. She would search out God and demand from him an explanation of all the sorrows of her life. God was in heaven, and she must climb up there somehow, and she tried hard to do it. She cut down some of the tall forest trees, and put them one on top of another, so as to make a ladder up to heaven. She built a great structure, but just when the topmost trees seemed to be getting near the sky the supporting timbers rotted away and the whole pile came crashing down.

The woman was still determined to find God and thought of another way to get at him. If she could find the place where the earth ends and touches the sky, there must be a road to God from there. So she set out to travel from village to village and tribe to tribe. As she passed through each country people asked the purpose of her journey, and she replied that she was searching for God. They asked why she was doing this, and the old woman answered that all her family had died and left her alone, a deserted and friendless old woman. But people retorted that it was not strange to lose friends and relatives. She was no different from the rest of mankind, for all people suffer such bereavements. Leza, the Besetting One, sits on the back of all men and none can ever get free from him. So the old woman was unable to solve her problem and she never found the way to heaven but eventually went the way of all flesh herself.

A similar story, with a happier ending, is told by the Chaga people of Kenya. It concerns a man whose sons had all died and the father was angry with God. Going to a blacksmith he demanded the finest arrows and said that he was going to shoot God. Then he set out for the farthest edge of the world, to the place where the sun rises. There he found many paths, some leading to heaven and some to earth. He stood waiting for the sunrise, and after a time heard the sound of many feet and people shouting that the gate must be opened for the king. The man saw a great host of shining people, and hid himself in fear. The Shining One was in the midst and many others followed after. Suddenly the procession stopped and people in front complained of a horrible smell, as if an earth man had passed that way. They looked around, found the Chaga man, seized him, and took him to God. God asked him what he wanted, and he replied that it was only sorrow that drove him from home, and he wanted to die in the bush. But God replied that he had heard the man wanted to shoot him, so let him shoot now. The man refused, and said that God knew what he wanted without asking. God answered that if he wanted his sons back he could take them, there they were standing behind him. The man looked and saw his sons, but they were so radiant that he hardly knew them, and he said that now they belonged to God and he must keep them.

Then God told the man to go home, but on the way he must look carefully and he would find something that would please him very much. On the road back he found a great store of elephants' tusks, and was made rich for life. And other sons were born to him and they lived to support their father in his old age. Other stories of visits to the world beyond usually have some promise of good fortune on the way home, if the divine instructions are obeyed.

No King as God

This proverb is one of the most popular in everyday use in West Africa today. It is often painted as a text on the front of motor lorries, to show that God is supreme and the human will must bow to him. The origin of the proverb is given in a Hausa story from Nigeria, but it resembles similar ones in both Europe and the East, as well as other parts of Africa.

When an ordinary man comes before a king he says, 'May the king live for ever'. But once upon a time there was a man who would say each time he came to court, 'There is no king like God'. He kept on saying this till the king got angry and plotted to destroy him. He gave the man two silver rings and told him they were a present to keep, but in reality the king meant to avenge himself through them. The man, whom everybody now called, No-King-as-God, took the rings, put them into a dried and empty ram's horn, and gave them to his wife to keep for him. A week later the king called No-King-as-God and sent him to a distant village, to tell the people to come and help build up the city walls. As soon as he had gone the king sent to the man's wife and offered her a million cowries (small imported shells used as currency and ornament), and a hundred head cloths and body-cloths, if she would give him that which her husband had entrusted to her. Tempted by the splendid presents the wife agreed and brought the ram's horn, and when the king looked inside there were two rings safely stored. He replaced them in the horn, and gave it to his servants with instructions to throw it far into a lake that never dried up. They did so, and as the horn fell into the water a great fish swam by and swallowed it up.

On the day that No-King-as-God was returning home he met some friends who were going fishing. He went with them and caught the great fish. As his son was cleaning it his knife struck something hard and he called his father. The father pulled out the horn, and when he opened it and looked inside he saw the rings which the king had given him for safe keeping. 'Truly', he said, 'there is no King like God'. They were still bathing when a royal messenger came and told the man he was wanted by the king at once. So he asked his wife where was that precious thing he had entrusted to her. She replied readily that she could not find it and thought a rat had eaten it.

Then the man set off for the royal court. The other councillors all saluted by saying, 'May the king live for ever'. But the man said only, 'There is no King like God'. So the king told the councillors to be quiet, and advancing towards the man he said, 'Is it true that there is no King like God?' The man replied firmly, 'Yes'. Then the king demanded that thing which he had entrusted to the man, and his guards closed round him to kill him. But No-King-as-God put his hand under his robe and pulled out the horn and handed it to the king. The king opened it and took out his two silver rings. 'Indeed, there is no King like God', he said, and all his councillors shouted in approval. Then the king divided his city into two, and gave half of it to No-King-as-God to rule.

Bronze bracelet from Dahomey representing a two-headed snake. Such rings are worn as lucky charms, and smaller snake rings are put on fingers to protect the wearer against snake bites in the hoeing season, on the theory that snake will not bit snake. The round snake symbolises life, continuity and eternity.

Left: royal calabash from Cameroun covered with patterns of coloured beads and sometimes used to hold the bones of ancestors. Other beaded calabashes are used as musical instruments—filled with seeds and shaken to accompany songs and dances. Horniman Museum.

Right: in many lands women suffer for the sake of beauty but rarely as much as the Ibo women of eastern Nigeria who traditionally wore large platelike gold anklets from adolescence. They were fixed and removed by smiths and when walking the legs had to be swung outwards, but a procession of ladies made a fine sight flashing in the sun. Other women wore copper anklets or spirals of brass which covered most of their legs. Horniman Museum.

Right, below: Personal decoration is dear to most African peoples, and some of them are masters in the making of it. Worn with pleasure by men and women alike, it increases in art and intricacy with the status of the wearer. The bracelet and beads are from Uganda, the necklace is Zulu work. Horniman Museum.

God Leaves the World

One of the best known of all African myths, found in many parts of the continent, tells of God leaving the world. It is generally agreed that in the earliest times God lived on earth but, generally due to some human fault, God got angry and went up to heaven. There is some idea of a Golden Age in the past, when God and man's ancestors were closer together, and some resemblance to the Bible story of the Garden of Eden, though there it is men who are expelled from the paradisal state. Some ancient Egyptian and classical myths told of the separation of sky and earth by their children, but although in the African stories God is almost identified with the sky, there are important differences in the various accounts.

The Mende people of Sierra Leone say that God made everything, heaven and earth, and animals, and last of all he made men and women. He told them that they could have whatever they wanted if they asked him. So when men were in need they demanded this or that, and God always gave it to them. But men came so often that they thought God's name must be just 'Take it!', which he said when they asked him for anything. And God grew tired of people troubling him so often, and saw that they would wear him out with their demands. So he decided to make himself a dwelling-place far away and above men. While men slept God went away and when they woke they could not find him. But then they looked up and saw God spread out in all directions, and they said that God was great. God said farewell to men, but warned them not to do evil to one another, for he had made men to live in agreement. Then he went up on high, and men call him 'High'. God also gave man and woman a fowl each, so that they might sacrifice to him if they did wrong to one another. So men still sacrifice and call on God to come down when they offer him a fowl in reparation for wrongdoing.

Along the west coast, in the Ivory Coast, Ghana, Togo, Dahomey and Nigeria there are common myths of God retiring from the earth. In olden days God lived very near men, in the sky, but just above their heads. He was so close that men grew familiar with him. Children would wipe their greasy hands on the sky when they finished their meals. Women, in search of an extra ingredient for dinner, would tear a piece off the sky and put it in the cooking pot. Especially women would knock against the sky when pounding their meal. This is one of the great female occupations of Africa, where mechanical flour mills have not been introduced. The grain is pounded in a wooden mortar, a scooped out piece of log, and a long wooden pestle is thumped down on the grains of corn. It is said that there was a woman once who had a very long pestle, and whenever she pounded her corn the wooden pole hit against God who lived just above the sky. One day she gave a great bang, hitting God in the eye, and in anger he went away to the distance where he has been ever since. This meant that people could no longer approach God so easily as before. The woman tried to get over this difficulty by telling her children to collect all the wooden mortars that they could find. These were all piled one on top of another and nearly reached up to heaven. Just one more mortar was needed, but they could not find one. So the old

The great Earth Mother of the Ibo people was propitiated annually at an increase ceremony. Elaborate headdresses were made for the occasion but the ceremony was abandoned at the end of the nineteenth century.

woman told her children to take the lowest mortar out from the bottom and put it on the top. When they did this all the other mortars fell down and many people were killed. The Ila story will be recalled, of the old woman who tried to pile up trees to reach heaven, like a Tower of Babel (see page 29).

It is remarkable that right across the other side of Africa similar stories are told. The Nuba people of the Sudan say that in the beginning the sky was low down and close to the earth, in fact it was so near that man could touch it. Women found that it pressed so low that they could not lift up their spoon high enough to stir their millet porridge, and their hands were forced to touch the pots and got burnt. One day a woman got angry at the pressure of the sky and gave her spoon a hard thrust upward. It went right through the sky. Then the sky was angry and retired to the distance where it has been ever since. Another version says that the sky was formerly so near that when people were hungry they tore pieces off the clouds to eat. Then the woman stabbed at the clouds with her spoon, and in anger at both these insults the sky moved away; and for this reason also the clouds only give their rain during one short season of the year. It will be noted that women are usually blamed for the disaster, as in the Genesis story, perhaps because the stories were told by men.

The Dinka people, also of the eastern Sudan, say that because the sky at first was so low, men and women had to be careful in hoeing the ground or pounding the grain not to touch God. Death had not yet come into the world, and God had given the first man and woman one grain of millet each day. This was enough for them and they were forbidden to grow or use any more. But one day the woman was greedy and chose to pound more grain than the ration. To do this she had to take a longer pestle, and when she raised it up she hit the sky, and so God went far away. Since that day men have had to work hard for their food, they are often hungry, they cannot reach God easily, and illness and death have come to them.

Another Dinka story explains the separation of God from man by saying that once there was a wall in heaven and this held man in the sky. But eventually man ate part of the wall and God pushed him down to earth. A more elaborate version says that the earth was already created, but it could not be seen because there was no light. So God created a man and pushed him to an opening in the heavenly wall, and then pulled him back. God gave the man eyes so that he could know that he was in the dark, and the man made a rope with which he caught an animal. He gave a leg of the animal to God's wife, who said he should be rewarded. When God asked the man what he wanted, he asked for a chink to see through. God refused this but he did present him with an axe. One day the man struck the earth with his axe and it lit up. God was angry at this and pushed the man down to earth.

A theme that is soon introduced, and often occurs, is that of a rope hanging from the sky, by which some men can get up to and down from heaven. The Dinka say that such a rope hung originally within reach of man who could climb up it to God. But when the woman had offended God by hitting the sky, God sent a blue bird to cut the rope so that men could not get to him easily. The Nuer people of the Sudan say that when men grew old they could climb up to the sky by a rope and become young again, and then they could return to earth and take up their life afresh. But one day the hyena – who often appears in the mythology of death – and a weaver-bird climbed up the rope to heaven. God saw them,

A standing female figure in painted wood, nursing a child and wearing the double-headed axe insignia of the Shango cult figures. Yoruba work.

35

and knowing that they might cause trouble, he gave orders that these two creatures were not to be allowed to go down to earth again. However the animals managed to escape one night, they climbed down the rope, which the hyena cut when they got near the earth. The part that was above the cut was then drawn up to heaven, and since then men have never been able to climb up to heaven and death has taken them away.

Many of the central and southern African peoples who speak of God as Mulungu say that he lived on earth at first, but went up to heaven by a spider's thread because men had begun to set fire to the bush and killed his people. Some say that when God was leaving the earth he could not climb a tree, which seems to have been the usual way up to the sky. So he went to the spider, who could get up and down again easily, and God went up to heaven on a spider's thread. In later stories people sometimes climb up to heaven by a rope or thread hanging from the clouds, like the long spider's webs that are seen on misty mornings, spun between great trees.

Another kind of story is told in Burundi in central Africa. In olden days God lived among men, talking with them, going from one to another, and creating the children that were born to them. But one day God created a crippled baby and its parents were angry. They plotted to take God unawares and stab him with a knife. But God, who sees all things, knew about the plot. He decided that if men were going to behave offensively he would return to heaven and show himself no more. In that way he could perform his acts of creation as he pleased and not be bothered by complaints from men. So he departed, and did not reveal himself again. But a few people have caught a glimpse of God, almost by accident and good fortune.

The Lozi (Barotse) people of the upper Zambesi in Zambia say that in the beginning God created the earth and all living creatures. At that time God and his wife lived here below among men. There was a man called Kamonu who was very clever, and imitated God in all that he did. When God worked in iron so did Kamonu, and when God forged Kamonu did so too. God began to be rather concerned, and when Kamonu made a spear and killed a large antelope God rebuked him, saying that he was killing his brothers, and drove him out. However Kamonu pleaded to return and God allowed him to cultivate land. Some time later buffaloes broke into Kamonu's plantation and he killed one of them, and when deer came he killed them also. Misfortune then befell his family; he broke a pot, his dog died, and his own child died. Kamonu went to complain about his losses to God and was surprised to see that his pot, dog and child were there with him. He asked for medicine to take them back, but God refused. Then God told his counsellors and his wife that since Kamonu had found his way to their dwelling they must move, and they went to live on an island in a river. But Kamonu made a raft and reached them. Next God made a great mountain and lived on top of it, but still Kamonu followed him.

God could not get away from men and they were multiplying everywhere. He sent out birds to find a place where he could get right away, but they were unsuccessful. He called his diviner, the wagtail, and asked him to throw the divining bones to find a refuge. The diviner found that they must ask the spider. So at the order of God the spider spun a thread which reached right up to the sky, and God and his family climbed up there and have stayed above ever since. But on the advice of the diviner the eyes of the spider were put out, so that it could not follow them up to the sky. Kamonu continued his efforts to reach God. Like the old

Left: headdress of a Yoruba king in Dahomey. Many rulers wore such crowns with beads hanging down in front of the face to add mystery and to emphasize their sacredness. But kings were not absolute, they could be removed from office, and were always subordinate to the spiritual world. A well known story and proverb declares that there is 'No King as God'.

Ancestral figure of the Fang of Gabon, some of the greatest African masters of sculptured form. Such figures are attached to gables over doors or put in a bark reliquary containing skulls of ancestors. Reproduced by kind permission of J. R. Hewitt, Esq.

The snake of eternity, with its tail in its mouth, apparently swallowing itself, yet with no beginning or end, like a circle or a sphere. This symbol is common in African art, painted on walls, woven in cloth, and worked in metal and wood. This clay moulding, or bas relief, is from the walls of the palace of King Ghezo of Dahomey, now a museum. It is regularly repaired and painted white, with red and blue rings round the neck.

Ila women he and his men cut down many trees and piled them on top of one another, trying to reach the sky. But the weight was too heavy and they all fell down. So every day when the sun rises men still salute God, and when the new moon appears they salute his wife.

There is a Pygmy story, perhaps influenced by negro myth, that formerly God lived on earth with his children, two boys and a girl (see page 50). But although he lived among them, they did not see God and were forbidden to try and look at him. He lived in a big house, where they heard him working at a smithy. The daughter was told to bring firewood every day and a pot of water, and leave them at the door of God's house. For a long time she had been curious, and one day she hid herself round the corner of the divine hut. She saw a big arm come out to take the pot, adorned with rich metal bracelets. But God knew that he had been seen and he called all his children together, and said that because of human disobedience he was going to leave them and move far away. He left them arms and tools so that they could look after themves. The girl he told to marry her brothers and give birth to children. Her first child died two days after its birth and death entered the world.

Animal figures from Ashanti, Ghana, used in weighing gold, are in many different forms, human, animal, fish, bird, insect or abstract. Many are 'proverb' weights to illustrate situations in life. An animal with long horns may be called, 'Had I known that, but it has passed behind me.' It is like the animal's horns, behind it, and means that regrets are vain when a thing is past.

The First Men

Probably all African peoples have traditions of their first ancestors, and these may also be mentioned in myths of God or legends of history.

The Zulu of South Africa used to say that the first human pair, a man and a woman, came out of a reed or a reed-bed. The Thonga of Mozambique said that one man and one woman came suddenly out of a reed, which exploded and there they were. It was long the custom to put a reed in the ground outside the house in which a baby was born. The Herero of South-west Africa say that their ancestors came out of a certain tree which is still thought to exist in the veld. Their cattle too came out of this tree, since they used to be great stock-breeders and lived close to the herds. But sheep and goats are said to have emerged from a hole in the ground. They said also that the small Bushmen came out of this hole, though in olden days the Bushmen had no sheep or goats themselves.

One of the versions of the origins of men current among the Ashanti of Ghana says that the first men came up to the surface from holes in the ground. Some say that on a Monday night, which is still significant in the seven-day week to certain groups of people, a worm made a passage up through the earth. There came up seven men, some women, a dog and a leopard; the latter is still sacred to some clans. The names of the men and women are still recounted by some old people, on Mondays or Tuesdays only. When the men and women looked around them on the face of the earth, they were very frightened at the strange sights there. Only their leader, Adu Ogyinae, was not afraid. On the Tuesday he calmed the fears of his friends by laying his hands on each of them. But when they began to build houses, on Wednesday, the leader was killed by a tree falling on him. Next the dog went out to look for some fire and brought it back to the men. They cooked some food, tried it on the dog first, and then ate it themselves. The God of creation was travelling about the world in his task of making things, and it seems that he met these people who had come up from the ground and took one of them to act as his helper and spokesman. His staff was long treasured by his relatives. There are still pots in the forest which are used for libations at annual ceremonies held in remembrance of these first people.

It has already been told that the Yoruba of Nigeria believe that the first men had been made in heaven and sent to earth with the help of Great God. The first man was giver of morality and family order, and he has been respected as ancestor and lawgiver ever since. He imposed taboos and punished anybody who broke them. His tutelary deity was Great God, since he had formed his body. Some of the other gods came down to earth, and of one of them it is said that he did not pay his respects to the first man but acted with disdain towards him. The man took his revenge by poisoning this god's daughter. Every effort was made to heal the girl but without success, and so at last the god came begging to man to heal him. The man was skilled in medicine, and demanded respect and repentance from the god before healing his daughter. The god yielded and gave him this, thus recognizing also the primacy of Great God who protected man.

The Shilluk of the upper Nile regions of the Sudan say that in the

A female ancestor figure from the Dogon people of Mali. Carved wood. Margaret Plass Collection.

beginning men lived in the land of God, but they ate fruit which made them sick and so God sent them away. This may suggest the Bible story, but it is found among tribes that seem to have had no Christian or Moslem influence. Another story says that in the olden days men used to be able to get up to the Moon by a road, but they became too heavy and could no longer use it. More commonly it is said that men and animals formerly lived together and were no different from one another. In those days there was no death, for cattle trampled on people

A door from a royal palace in Dahomey, with wooden figures nailed to it. Below is a snake swallowing its tail, and above a chameleon between the sun and moon. A Nigerian myth says that when God created the earth he sent the chameleon to inspect it, and after walking about slowly it reported that the earth was not yet dry enough. A Zulu myth blames the chameleon for coming too slowly to men, with the message from God that they would not die. The lizard raced ahead and told men that they would die, and so death came.

when they were old and they became young again. Then the stories connect the first people with their more historical ancestors, but still with mythological details. The founder of the Shilluk royal house, Nyikang, was the son of a man who came from heaven, or perhaps he was a being specially created in the form of a cow. Anyway he married a woman who was a crocodile, or a river creature who had the attributes of a crocodile, though as the myth develops she appears as a woman. This crocodile-woman represents all the beings of the rivers, and offerings are still made to her at grassy spots on river banks where crocodiles emerge. If any water animal acts in an unusual way it is still looked on as a temporary incarnation of the original woman. She is regarded as the patron of birth and protector of babies.

The Dinka of the Sudan says that the first man and woman, Garang and Abuk, were made very small of clay and put in a pot, but when it was opened they became big. These were the people to whom God gave one grain of corn a day, till Abuk was greedy and pounded more. Garang is also a power, or 'free-divinity', which falls on men from the sky and enters their body, becoming their divinity. Such 'men of Garang' often wear leopard-skins, and as they are thought to be powerful doctors their hands are covered with rings and bracelets which mothers give them to cure their children. Garang is sometimes associated with a snake, of red and white colour, and other animals which have white in association with red or brown are emblems of Garang: such as giraffes and oxen, and there is a tree with yellow-brown fruit. These colours also associate Garang with the sun. Abuk was the primeval woman, whose greed and offence against the sky are viewed indulgently when the story is told. She is connected with the waters and her emblem is a small snake. Abuk is patron of women and their produce, the gardens and the grain used for brewing beer, for which women are responsible.

Many stories are told in Buganda, Uganda, of Kintu the first man and ancestor. When he came to the country from the gods he lived by himself with only one cow and lived on her milk. Then a woman Nambi came and fell in love with him, but she had to go back to her father, Gulu, who was king of heaven. Nambi's relatives despised Kintu because he knew of no food but milk and they objected to the marriage. To test him Gulu robbed Kintu of his cow and the man had to live on herbs and leaves. But Nambi saw the cow, and went and told Kintu that it was in heaven and invited him to fetch it.

When Kintu arrived he was surprised to see many cows, sheep, fowls and houses there. In the meantime Nambi's brothers told their father that Kintu had arrived and a test was arranged for him. A huge meal was cooked, enough for a hundred people, and Kintu was told that unless he ate it all he would be killed. He was shut up in a house with the food, and when he had eaten his fill he did not know what to do with the rest. Then he discovered a hole in the floor so he dropped all the food and beer into it, and called the people to take away the empty baskets. Gulu could hardly believe that Kintu had eaten all the food, and fixed a further test. He sent him a copper axe and told him to cut firewood from the rock, because he did not use ordinary wood. But Kintu found a rock with cracks in it, so he broke them off and returned to Gulu. Yet another trial was imposed, and Kintu was told to fetch water which must be dew only. He took the pot into a field and put it down while he thought what to do, but to his surprise when he went to the pot it was full of dew.

Gulu was so impressed that he thought Kintu was a wonderful being,

A dance mask of the Epa society of the Yoruba. The dancer's head was enclosed by the hollow 'face' which formed the base and rested on the shoulders. The whole measured three feet in height.

41

THE FIRST MEN

Calabash from the Hausa of northern Nigeria. This gourd cut in two is used in temples for receiving offerings, and it also symbolizes heaven and earth. The top is that inverted bowl we call the sky; the earth is below or floating inside like a small calabash in a large one. The lips where the bowls join represent the horizon. Many calabashes are decorated with patterns of snakes, animals, men or gods. British Museum.

Snakes and tortoises are frequently carved in Africa, as in this Yoruba panel from Nigeria. In a myth of neighbouring Dahomey a coiled snake supports the earth, with 3,500 coils above and 3,500 coils below. The snake is also said to have erected four pillars to hold up the sky, and coiled itself round the pillars to keep them upright.

42

and agreed to let him marry his daughter. He told Kintu to pick out his own cow from the herds, but this was not easy because there were many others just like his own. Just then a large bee flew up and told Kintu to choose the cow on whose horns it alighted. In the morning, when the cows were brought Kintu kept his eye on the bee, which stayed in a tree. He said that his cow was not in the herd. When a second herd was brought he said the same. In the third herd the bee landed on a large cow, and Kintu claimed it as his own. The bee went on to settle on three calves, which Kintu said had been born during the cow's stay in heaven. Gulu was delighted, and declared that since nobody could deceive Kintu he could take his daughter Nambi as wife. The story of Nambi and death is told later.

In Malagasy it is said that in the beginning the Creator made two men and a woman, and all lived on earth, but separately, knowing nothing of each other. The first man carved a woman out of wood, full-size, and was so enamoured of it, like Pygmalion, that he talked to the image all the time and put it in the open so that he could look at it while he worked. One day the second man, walking through the bush, came upon the statue and was struck by its beauty, but its nakedness shocked him and he covered it with beautiful clothing and jewels. Later the woman came along, lamenting her solitude, and when she saw the image she fell down on her knees and asked the Creator to give it life. He promised to do so if she would take it to her bed.

She clasped the image tightly all night and in the morning it was alive as a beautiful girl. Then the two men came up and claimed the girl as their handiwork. The woman refused to give her up and God had to intervene. He decreed that the first man was father of the girl, since he had made the image from wood. The woman was its mother, since she had given it life. The second man should be the girl's husband, since he had adorned her with so much love. This arrangement was accepted, and of course the first man married the woman, while the second man married the girl. From these two couples descend everybody on earth today. From the first man came the clan of sculptors, and all men must give clothing and ornaments to their wives.

Another Malagasy story says that in the beginning the woman, the cow and the bitch were all children of the same father and lived together. One day God wanted a servant for his throne and sent fever down to earth to get a life from the woman. Her only child became sick and she sent for her relatives to bring all the medicinal plants they could find. But these were no use and the child got worse. During the night God appeared to the woman with a great knife in his hand uplifted to strike. She fell on her knees and begged for mercy. God said he would spare her if she gave him a life in place of that of her child. In the morning the woman went to the bitch, who was the elder, and asked for help to meet the divine demands. The bitch agreed at first, but when the woman told her dream, and the bitch saw that she wanted one of her litter, she refused, telling the woman to die herself for the child. The woman went to the cow with the same request, and moved with pity the cow gave her the younger and weaker calf of the two that she had. The woman quickly killed it and offered it to God. Her own child opened its eyes and recovered. Then the woman swore that she and her children would always take care of the cow and its young, and look on them as the most faithful companions. But they would not look after dogs, and even though they came from the same parents dogs would always be servants. That is why dogs run in front of man, for they are older, but

A carved wooden dance mask of the Senufo people of the Ivory Coast, showing a chameleon and a hornbill on a head which combines the horns of an antelope with the features of a warthog. The chameleon is a creature which often features in the myths of Africa.

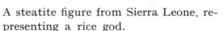

A steatite figure from Sierra Leone, representing a rice god.

they have to wait for their masters; they are the lowest of domestic animals and are not allowed to enter houses.

The Luyia of Kenya say that when God had created the sun he wondered for whom it would shine. So he made the first man, called Mwambu. Since the man could talk and see he needed a companion, and God made the first woman, whose name was Sela. They wanted something to drink, so God made water fall from heaven which filled up the holes and valleys to make lakes and rivers. God instructed Mwambu and Sela in the flesh they could eat, some animals were allowed for food but others were taboo. They were forbidden to eat crawling beasts like snails and lizards, or birds that feed on carrion like hawks and vultures. One day God surprised a buffalo cow with its young, and it ran away leaving the young ones, which were male and female. God took them and gave them to the man and woman. They fed them on an ant-hill, and some people say that originally cattle came from an ant-hill. Mwambu and Sela lived in a house supported by posts, because they were afraid of earthly monsters. Their children came down and lived on the ground, but tree-houses are still used sometimes in forests, and houses on piles stand in the waters at the edge of lakes.

Another Luyia story says that in the olden days people had no knowledge of making pots, they simply used calabashes which grew wild, and which many people cultivate now. It was the children who were responsible for finding how to make pots. They saw their mothers with fine calabashes, which they had gathered in the bush, and children tried to make some for themselves, with bits of clay in the shape of calabashes. Somehow their clay pots got in the fire, and they found that if they got

Left: stylised representation of a snake from the Baga people of Guinea. A single piece of wood six feet tall carved and painted. One myth says that all water on earth was still, until the serpent came and traced the courses for the rivers; thus the world received life.

A spirit figure from the Bayaka of the Congo. The shape of the nose is characteristic of the region. These spirit figures are much used, enhanced by medicine and spells, to control the forces of nature.

hard the water would not leak out as it did when the pots were wet. So children made the first clay pots, and when mothers saw they were good they copied them and made bigger pots for their own use. These large pots were made of damp clay at first and they collapsed. They could not be used till they had been put in the fire and hardened, as the children had done.

Some women are wholly given to special tasks and are freed from the housework that most women do. The Luyia say that this happened first when two sisters lived together. One was so busy making pots all the time that she left all other work to her sister. The sister was so annoyed that she broke all the pots. Then the pot-maker was angry and ran away from home. She went for three days on foot till she reached a big lake and saw a tall tree in the middle. The tree noticed the girl at the water's edge and came towards her so that she could climb up into its branches, and then it went back again into the water. The woman's parents had been looking for her everywhere and at last they reached the lake. They saw her sitting in the top of the tree in the middle of the water. They could not get to her and called out, begging her to come home. The girl refused to do this, till at last her lover came and called her too. Then she agreed to return to the shore, on condition that she could do her work without trouble. Her parents agreed, made her some new pots, and excused her all housework so that she never had to do any more.

A Pygmy story of the first men links it with that character who often appears in fable, the chameleon. Once upon a time a chameleon heard some whispering in a tree, like birds chirping or water running. That was surprising since there was no water on earth at that time. The Chameleon took an axe and cut open the trunk of the tree, till at last water came out, in a great flood that spread all over the earth. With this water emerged the first human couple, a woman and a man. Both were light-skinned, like the lightest-coloured of the Pygmies. As there were no other people on earth, this couple lived together and gave birth to the first child. Another Pygmy story says that three people were created first (see page 50).

There is a Pygmy story of the first man, called Efé. God had placed him on earth, but after a time he wanted him to come back to heaven as a hunter. He cut a long liana and drew Efé up to heaven by it. He gave him three spears and told him to go hunting. Efé killed an elephant, whose tusks were as big as great trees. All the people of heaven were happy, especially the women, who embraced the hunter before cutting up the elephant. Efé stayed for a long time hunting in the sky, but finally he was sent back to earth, taking his three spears and many presents. All the Pygmy camp gathered round for his arrival but nobody recognized him, after his long absence he was a stranger. At last his brother came up and said that even if he should die he would try to find out who the stranger was. Eventually he identified Efé, and asked where he had been for so long. Efé replied that he had been with their father in the sky. 'Is he still alive?' asked the brother. Efe said, 'Yes, and he has sent us these spears and presents'. Then everybody embraced him and rejoiced.

The mythology of the first men told by the Dogon of the Upper Volta is long and complex, following on their creation stories. The first man and woman created bore a series of twins, who were the ancestors of the Dogon tribe. The four eldest ancestors were males and the others females. The oldest ancestor after a time went to the ant-hill or womb

A wooden mask covered with wire, representing the first ancestor of the Dogon of Mali. The first ancestor stole fire from the heavenly blacksmiths, and slid down a rainbow with it so fast that he broke his sinuous arms and legs, and since then men have had joints at elbows and knees.

of the primeval mother and disappeared into it.

The only trace that remained was a wooden bowl on the ground which he had worn as a hat to protect him from the sun. The ancestor was led by the male Nummo spirit (see page 23) into the depths of the earth, where he shrank to the form of seed, like water, and when it was perfected it rose up to heaven. The eight ancestors were transformed in this way and went to heaven where the Nummo reigned, the first pair. But special change occurred with the seventh ancestor. Seven is a perfect number, being the union of four which is feminine and three which is masculine. The seventh ancestor received knowledge of a Word, which brought progress to mankind and enabled it to get ahead of the jackal, who had taken the first Word. The seventh ancestor revealed his Word by the art of weaving. It was also seen, from the bowl which the ancestors left behind, and by studying the ant-hill, how to make better dwellings than the caves in which they had formerly lived.

Up in heaven, however, things were not going well. The eight ancestors were transformed into the same essence as the Nummo pair, but the Nummo were chiefs and they separated the ancestors from one another and forbade them to come together, so as to keep the peace. God had given the ancestors eight different grains each for food; but when all were eaten except the last, the first and second ancestors came together to eat it. So they disobeyed the Nummo orders and became unclean. They then determined to leave heaven and the other ancestors joined them. With the help of God they took with them whatever might be useful on earth.

The first ancestor took a basket and some clay, which was particularly important, as it was a model for the world system. It was moulded with clay on a basket framework, upside down, but when inverted it had a circular base, a square top, and four sides in which were staircases each of ten steps. The circular base stood for the sun, and the square top the sky; in this roof there was a circle for the moon. The stairs were male and female, and together they denoted the children of the ancestors. They were also associated with men, animals, birds, insects, and stars. This primeval construction was like a granary and was called the Granary of the Master of Pure Earth. It contained compartments, like an earthly granary, for different seeds which God gave the eight ancestors. They also symbolize the organs of the human body.

The story has been told of the first ancestor stealing fire from the Nummo blacksmith. When the Nummo hurled a thunderbolt the first ancestor loosed the granary and it came down a rainbow to earth, with increasing speed from the blows of thunder and lightning. When it landed with a crash the men, animals and vegetables were scattered about. The ancestor came down from the roof of the granary by the steps. He marked out land for fields and distributed it among the descendants of the ancestors. The first ancestor was a smith, and the others began the work and arts of leather-workers, minstrels, and so on. There was trouble with a snake. Some say it was the seventh ancestor and others that it was the granary itself. Anyway the snake was killed and its head buried under a stone in the smithy. It may represent the original granary which was spread abroad on crashing to earth.

The Dogon say that for the purposes of God men had now to be organized. They lived in eight families, descended from the eight ancestors. The eighth family was regarded as superior, since it had Speech. The oldest man was called Lebe and he represented the Word. But he had to die, or at least appear to die, though Death had not yet come to

The art of the Ijaw of the Niger Delta
is noted for its cubist quality. This figure, called Ejiri, is an impersonal means
of controlling life and gaining success.
The steed is probably a leopard, with a
fierce mouth but with human faces on
its legs.

Wooden statue of a chimpanzee from the Congo. A Pygmy story says that the chimpanzees were the first to possess fire, and when a Pygmy saw it in their village he planned to take it home. He went in a long bark-cloth and sat so close to the chimpanzees' fire that the cloth set alight and he dashed home with the fire. The chimpanzees gave chase but could not catch him. They complained that the Pygmy had stolen the fire instead of buying it honestly, and they left their village and went to live in the forest without fire.

Right: the mythical buck of the Bambara of Mali was sent by the Creator to teach men how to cultivate corn. The cotton robe is painted with patterns symbolizing the universe. The masqueraders dance in pairs in the fields to ensure fertility of crops and families.

earth. He was buried lying on his back, with his head to the north. He was swallowed by the seventh ancestor who had taken the form of a snake. Then the snake vomited stones in the shape of a body, like the outlines of a man's soul. The stones were placed in order, one for the head, eight principal stones for each ancestor marking the joints, and then secondary stones filled in the ribs, spine and bones. These stones were symbolical of the life-force of the eight ancestors, sent into their descendants and kept later by priests. The arranging of the stones of the joints helped to fix the social system, especially marriages, in which there is alternation of left and right, upper and lower. So the eighth man's body symbolized both man and society. He was swallowed so that men should know that his bones had been transformed and that he was present in these covenant-stones. From Lebe, having been swallowed, all that was good from the former Word was put into the stones, and all that was impure was cast away. This was only done in appearance, since Lebe was not really dead or eaten, but it was done for mankind, to give life-force to men. There is a great annual sacrifice to Lebe, a victim on behalf of mankind.

The shape of the Dogon house is also explained symbolically. The floor is like the Earth, and Lebe who was restored to life in the earth. If it is placed correctly then the door is open towards the north, and at the opposite end is the hearth, where cooking pots are supported on two stones and the rear wall. The two stones mark east and west, and the wall indicates south. The flat roof of the house is like heaven, in the Granary of the Master of Pure Earth. There may be four small roofs round the central roof, indicating the cardinal points of the compass. The rooms of the house symbolize male and female and their union. The vestibule is the male, while the big central room is the woman, with store-rooms at each side as her arms. The end room with the hearth is her head. The woman lies on her back, and the ceiling above is also the man. Four posts supporting the room are the arms of the man and woman entwined in the act of union. Thus the family house represents the union of man and woman. It also recalls the primeval union of God and Earth.

Like the house the Dogon village also should be orientated north to south, like a prostrate being, human or divine. The smithy should be at the head, like the family hearth. The family houses are in the centre, with women's and men's separate houses like hands on east and west. Millstones and a foundation altar are lower down like sexual organs, and other altars are the feet. Villages can only be arranged fully in this manner on the plains, for in hills the contours and rocks force other arrangements. But seen from the air, in the light of mythical explanation, both houses and villages take on a new significance.

Many other Dogon stories, too numerous to relate here, tell of the institution of agriculture, weaving, smithying, trade, dress and love. These are connected with the original myths of God, Earth, Nummo spirits, and the ancestors, and form explanatory patterns and justifications for human activities.

The Mystery of Birth

Another version of the Ashanti story of the origins of men (page 39) says that long ago a man and a woman came down from heaven, while another man and woman came out of the ground. The Lord of Heaven also sent a python, the non-poisonous snake, which made its home in a river. In the beginning men and women had no children, they had no desire for one another and did not know the process of procreation and birth. It was the python who taught them. He asked the men and women if they had any children, and on being told that they had none, the python said he would make the women conceive. He told the couples to stand facing each other, then he went into the river and came out with his mouth full of water. This he sprayed on their bellies, saying 'Kus, kus,' words that are still used in clan rituals. Then the python told the couples to go home and lie together, and the women conceived and bore children. These children took the spirit of the river where the python lived as their clan spirit. Members of that clan to this day hold the python as taboo; they must never kill it, and if they find a python that has died or been killed by someone else, they put white clay on it and bury it in almost human fashion. The symbolism of the snake is obvious and has been used in mythology at least since the book of Genesis.

A Pygmy story says that at first three people were created, two boys and a girl. One of the boys was a negro and the other a Pygmy. One day the negro told the Pygmy that he did not know what to do with his sister, for she was always bleeding despite all the medicines that he put on her wound. The Pygmy had already been told by God the meaning of this physical phenomenon and he laughed at the negro, saying he would cure the wound. So he took the girl and she bore him children. Then he returned the woman to her brother and explained to him the mystery of procreation as the cure for the female ill. Then the negro also begat children. Though later this would be regarded as incestuous, in myth it solves the problem of how the first pair had children.

Another Pygmy myth says that the Lightning lived with a woman, as brother and sister, for the way of procreation was not known to them. One day the Moon came to visit the Lightning and, seeing how he lived with the woman, advised him to consummate his marriage. The Lightning refused at first, because he did not know how to proceed. Then the Moon made monthly periods come to the woman. Some say that a young man took the woman first and showed the way. Anyway the Lightning plucked up courage and did the same. The first child was very

A Yoruba male twin figure. The Yoruba attribute an indivisible soul to twins, so the soul of a twin that dies must be given a permanent home in the sort of figure shown here. The figures are carefully guarded and duly blessed by the priest at the annual festival of twins.

A bronze from the Kwale division of the Ibo people of Nigeria, representing an anthropomorphic creature with a man's face. Two chameleons ride on his back. It was possibly used as a weight.

light-skinned but others were darker, and when at length the woman died the Moon took her up to the heavens where he lived with the Sun.

A Malagasy story says that one day a man was fishing when he felt a strong pull on his line. He drew it in carefully, thinking it to be a big fish. He was very frightened to see a woman emerge from the water, and he threw everything down to run away when the woman called out that he should not be afraid. She said she would marry him, only he must promise never to look at what was underneath her arm. The man agreed, they were married, and had a son and daughter. But when the children were growing up the husband could no longer resist the temptation to look in his wife's armpit, and he did this while she seemed to be asleep. The woman saw him and said nothing, but next day she suggested that they should go for a bathe. The man went into the water first, while his wife looked after the children on the bank. Then it was her turn, and as she disappeared into the waters she called out that she was leaving him, because he had broken her taboo. Some say that in her armpit she had an extra mouth. Others declare that the taboo was for her husband not to look at her while she was naked – he did this while she undressed and she gave a great cry and disappeared. Both versions may contain veiled allusions to the sex taboo, and the origins of procreation. The woman is claimed as mother of fishing clans.

A story of the Luyia of Kenya says that the first man and woman had no children for a long time. They did not know the secret of procreation and tried to have union in various ways but without success. One day the man saw his wife climbing into the granary and noticed her private parts, and so at night he sought union with her. She refused him at first, saying that he had only seen an ulcer, but later she gave in and suffered great pain. In due course she bore a son, much to the surprise of both parents. Later a girl was born to them.

Further mysteries of birth are children born with some abnormality, and they are usually feared. A baby born with an extra finger may be *sent back* – neglected or exposed on a river bank – after rites which separate his bad luck from the family. Then there are *born-to-die* children, from mothers who have had a succession of babies dying at birth, the same child is believed to be born each time. Stories tell of a child whose body is carefully marked at death; the same scar appears on the next child to be born.

Twins, and even more triplets, are regarded with mixed feelings of fear and joy, as abnormal, even animal, births. In eastern Nigeria they used to be exposed in pots in the forest. But in western Nigeria and Dahomey they are prized, as the gods themselves, it is believed, were born in pairs. Images of twins, now often sold as curios, were used for rituals, and in front of them offerings were placed in twin pots. If a twin dies the survivor, or the mother, wears a wooden image of the dead one tucked in the waist cloth. In Buganda twins were said to come from the great god Mukasa, and doctors made ceremonies to ensure health and prosperity. The Thonga of Mozambique called twins 'children of the sky', but thought their birth a great misfortune which needed rituals of purification. They were sent with their mother to live in a special hut outside the village and would not be popular even when grown up. But if storms threatened the village the twins were asked to intercede, since the sky would listen to its children. They stood outside the hut calling on the storm to go away, to thunder farther off and not annoy people. The mother of twins was credited with similar powers, since she had been up to the sky to get her twins and she could speak to it.

A wooden cylindrical drum of the Baulé of the Ivory Coast, decorated with copies of masks, figures, lizards, hands, rosettes and abstract patterns, all of which add power to the drum.

Left: brass Kuduo box from Ashanti, Ghana. A ceremonial vessel in which offerings are placed when 'washing the soul' and remembering the first people of the clan. It was buried with its owner, along with gold dust and beads. The decorative cover shows a leopard attacking a deer.

Right: the Hare is one of the most popular and cunning animals in African fable and is the original of Brer Rabbit whose stories were taken by African slaves to America. He represents the ordinary man faced with more powerful beings but often winning by his cleverness. In this Yoruba mask from Nigeria the Hare motif is plain, and he can be seen climbing up the back. British Museum.

Right, below: man, woman and snake are common themes in mythology, as shown in this carved and painted wooden bowl of the Yoruba, Nigeria. The snake is the sacred non-poisonous python, the round symbol of life and eternity, and in some stories it teaches man and woman the mystery of procreation. British Museum.

The Origins of Death

Several myths already related have mentioned the coming of death, and all over Africa stories are told which show the belief that death is unnatural and was not found among men in the beginning. Its coming is blamed on some mistake, often the fault of an animal, the dog or the chameleon.

The Messengers

The Kono of Sierra Leone say that in olden times there was the first man and woman and their baby boy. The Supreme Being told them that none of the three would die, but when they got old they would have new skins for their bodies. He put these new skins in a bundle and entrusted it to the dog to take to man. The dog went off with the bundle, but on the way he met other animals who were feasting on rice and pumpkins. They invited the dog to join them and he put down his burden and shared the feast. During the meal he was asked what was in his bundle and he told the story of the new skins that were being sent to men. But when the snake overheard this he slipped out quietly, stole the bundle and shared out the skins with other snakes. The dog had to confess to man that the skins had been stolen, and they both went to God. But it was too late, the snake kept the skins, and since then man has died. The snake was punished by being driven away from towns to live alone, and if a man finds a snake he tries to kill it.

The Mende of Sierra Leone give a different version, which is also widespread, about two messengers. The dog and the toad were sent to take messages to mankind about death; the dog to say that men would not die, and the toad to say they would. The animals set out together, but the dog stopped on the way. He met a woman who was preparing food for her child, and he waited till he got some for himself. The toad had continued without stopping and arrived at the town of men crying out, 'Death has come'. Just then the dog ran up crying, 'Life has come'. But it was too late.

The Nuba of the eastern Sudan say that, at first, when a man died, God told his relatives that he was only asleep; so they put him aside for the night and next morning he would be found alive again. But one day when a man died, and before God told men what to do, a hare came and told the relatives to bury the corpse in the ground, else God would be angry and would kill them all. So the relatives buried the man and when God came they told him what had been done. Then God was really angry that they had listened to the hare instead of to him, and he said that in future all men would die and not come back again.

A Nuer story says that when God created man he took a piece of a gourd and cast it into the water, as a sign that as the gourd floated so man would live for ever. Then God sent a barren woman to give men the message, but when she illustrated it in the same way, instead of throwing a buoyant gourd she cast a piece of earthen pot into the water and it sank. Since then men have died.

Calabash toy from Madagascar, decorated to represent a porcupine. The calabash is a gourd which grows above the ground like a marrow and can be forced into different shapes. When ripe the pulp inside is scooped out, and often dry seeds are put in to make a rattle used in music.

A pottery figure from Dahomey represents the Just King. On the left the King stretches out his hand in judgement, the condemned man waits in the middle with hands tied behind his back, while the executioner on the right lifts his axe.

Far left: symbolical swords are used in state and religious rituals, and this finely decorated one from Ashanti, Ghana, has abstract patterns as well as a snake and tortoise. The sword is carried in front of a chief, and a man swearing loyalty is handed the sword which he points to heaven and earth as his witnesses.

THE ORIGINS OF DEATH

Right: many African masks represent in realistic or stylised form the heads of animals which are believed to have great power, concentrated in the head. The wearer is protected from evil by this power and dances like the animal. This painted animal mask comes from the Bapende of the Congo. British Museum.

This male figure holding a bowl was used in making offerings to spirits by the Bafum of Cameroun.

A Dinka story gives the different explanation that men die because there is not room for them all. The first man and woman were created in the east, on the bank of a great water, under a tamarind tree. They were very small, half as long as a man's arm, made of clay, and laid in a pot. When the Creator took the top off the pot the man and woman stood up fully grown, with completely developed organs. They had children and he told them that they would die, but would come back after fifteen days. The man did not agree and said that if they came back there would be no room for them, no land to cultivate or build houses.

In Burundi it is said that in olden days Death was not among men and God still lived on earth. If Death happened to appear God chased him away with his hunting hounds. One day Death was being pursued closely by the divine dogs who forced him into a narrow place. He ran into a woman coming from the other direction and promised that if she hid him he would hide her and her family. The woman opened her mouth and Death jumped inside. Then God came along and demanded where Death had gone. The woman replied that she had not seen him. But God, who is the Seeing One and knows everything, knew what had happened. He told the woman that since she had hidden Death, in future Death would destroy her and all hers. God left the woman in anger and from that day death has spread among men.

A Luyia story says that in olden days people used to die, but after four days they came back to life. But one day a boy died and when he returned his mother sent him away, saying he was dead and ought to stay that way. The boy did go away, but in going he cursed the people, and said that in future those who died would not return.

A further Luyia story says that Maina, son of the ancestor of their people, was sitting outside his house one evening eating his meal after work. As he sat there the chameleon came and asked for some food. By the laws of hospitality Maina should have given some at once, but he refused. The chameleon asked again and again until Maina grew angry and drove the beast away. The chameleon cursed him and said that he would leave, but Maina and all his people would die. Then the chameleon went on and met the snake. He asked for food in the same way and the snake at once shared his food with him. So the chameleon blessed the snake and said he would live for ever. People began to breathe bad air, sicken and die, while the snake sheds its skin and goes on living.

Many Bantu peoples have stories in which the chameleon is associated with death. A Zulu myth says that God sent the chameleon to men with the message that they would not die. But the chameleon walks slowly and it ate fruit on the way. Some time later God sent the lizard saying that men should die. The lizard scuttled off, got there first, and gave his message and even returned to God before the chameleon had reached its destination. Men had accepted the word of the lizard and that could not be changed.

The Pandora's Box theme (see page 28) appears also in a story by the Lamba people of Zambia. The chief of men used to be a nomad, but finally he wanted to settle down and till the soil. He had no seeds, so he sent to God to ask for some. God gave his messengers little bundles, and one of them in particular they were told not to untie but to give it to their chief intact. The divine insistence on this point aroused the curiosity of the messengers, and when they stopped for the night on the road they began to untie the bundles, to see what God was sending their chief. When they opened the forbidden bundle death came out and spread into the world.

Rather different is a story of the Ila of Zambia. The first man and woman were given by God a choice between two little bags, one containing life and the other death. As one bag shone with a bright light the foolish parents chose this, which of course contained death, and a few days later one of their children died. However God gave the parents another chance, and when they begged him to restore the child to life he promised to do this, if they would refrain from eating for three days. But their hunger became so great that they could not hold out, they took some food, and ever since then death has come to mankind.

In Buganda the coming of death is connected with the myth of the first man Kintu and his heavenly wife Nambi (see page 41). As they were leaving the sky Gulu warned them to hurry because Death would want to go with them, and if they had forgotten anything they must not

An ivory mask representing a king of Benin, Nigeria, with a tiara of small heads depicting the Portuguese visitors who went to Benin from A.D. 1472. Such masks are still worn on ceremonial occasions by the King of Benin.

go back. They set out with cows, a goat, a sheep, a fowl and a plantain tree, a sort of banana. On the way Nambi said she had forgotten grain for the fowl and must go back for it. Kintu tried to dissuade her, but Nambi would not listen and returned to ask Gulu for grain. She tried to steal away, but her brother Death followed her, and Kintu was angry that Death had come. Nambi pacified him by saying they must go on and see what happened. When they got to the earth Nambi planted a garden, and she lived happily with her husband, bearing many children.

One day Death asked Kintu for one of his children to be his cook. Kintu refused, saying that if Gulu came he would be ashamed to say that one of his children was Death's cook. Death asked again, and when Kintu refused again he said he would kill the child. Kintu did not know what 'kill' meant, but the child soon sickened and died. After this other children died at intervals, and Kintu went up to heaven and complained about Death to Gulu. Gulu told him that he had been warned, and if he had not allowed Nambi to return for grain they would have been protected from Death. But after some entreaty Gulu sent Death's brother, Kaizuki, to stop Death killing all the children.

Kaizuki found Death and fought with him but Death managed to escape. Kaizuki told all the people to stay in their houses, with their animals, and he would prepare a last hunt for Death. He also said that if they saw Death they must not call out or make any noise. All went well, and Kaizuki had lured Death from his hiding place in the ground when some children came out with their goats. They saw Death and called out in fear, and at this Death went back into the earth. So Kaizuki told Kintu that he was tired of hunting Death, nothing could be done to catch him, and he himself was returning to heaven. Since then Death has lived on earth; he kills people when he can and then escapes into the ground.

A Malagasy myth says that God had a daughter called Earth, and she played at making little men out of clay. One day God saw the manikins and was interested. He blew into them and the clay images came to life. God told Earth to call them Velo-'living'. The Velo men multiplied and did not die. Soon the Earth prospered, for men worked on the land and produced fine harvests. Another day when God was standing on a high mountain he saw the prosperity of the Earth and was surprised, and perhaps jealous. He called Earth to his palace and demanded that she give him half of the men. But Earth pleaded with him that although everything belonged to God yet she could not be separated from her men, for they made her wealth. God was angry and said he would take away the breath of life that he had given to the Velo. He did this, and Earth wept, crying out, 'O lo Velo', meaning 'Men are decaying'. Since then men decay and die.

Another Malagasy story says that all the animals and birds met one day to see whether a remedy could be found against death, which was always reducing their numbers with unknown maladies. They decided that the kings of all the animals should pray to God to provide a cure for the mortal ill. He agreed to, and told the kings to assemble with all their subjects before a great building. They were to appoint the bull as a guard because the remedy against death would be inside. But God was delayed, and the animals began to drift away. Then the king of the bulls was overcome with hunger and thirst and looked around for something to sustain him. He found it inside the building – and when God arrived he found that the remedy itself had been drunk. Angry, he demanded to know who had done this thing. The snake, who had not gone far away and had seen what had happened, accused the bull of the theft.

A statue from Ifé, Nigeria, showing a royal figure. The face is probably carved from life but the shortened body is stylised and dressed in robes like those still used in coronation ceremonies. An axe in one hand and a horn in the other are symbols of power.

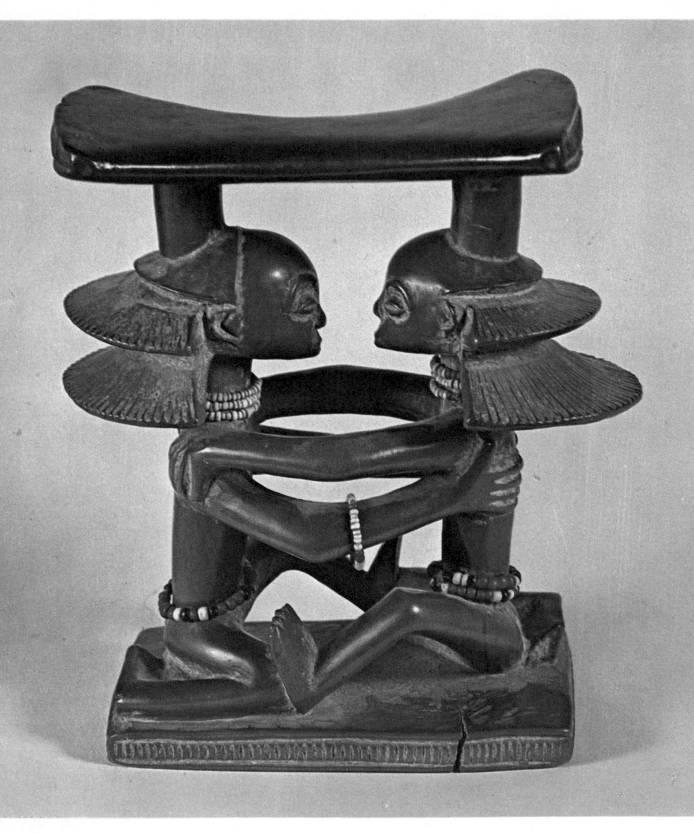

God said he would be punished; he recalled the other animals and told them that if they were ill they must get their remedy from the bull. That is why men sacrifice a bull when they are seriously ill.

A Death Giant

A different sort of explanation of death is given by the Krachi of Togo. In the beginning there was a famine on earth, and a young man wandering about the forest looking for food came to a place that was quite new to him. He saw a great lump on the ground, and when he reached it found that it was a giant covered with long silky hair. The hair was so long it would have stretched from one village to another. He tried to creep away but suddenly the giant looked up and asked him what he wanted. The lad said he was hungry and the giant promised to feed him if he became his servant. The youth agreed, and learnt that the giant's name was Death. The food was delicious and the young man was happy to serve Death for a long time. But eventually he got homesick and begged leave from the giant, who let him go on the promise that he would send another boy to serve in his place. He brought the giant his brother. The young man went home, but after a time he was hungry again, the famine being still severe, and he longed for the giant's fine food. He returned to the giant and was given as much food as he wanted, under the condition of working for him again. He stayed there a long time, but was surprised that he never saw his brother. When he asked Death about him he was told that the boy was away on some business.

In time the youth was homesick again and asked for another holiday. The giant agreed again, if he would bring him a girl to marry. The lad persuaded his sister to marry Death, and she accepted, taking a servant to her new home. Not long after he was hungry again and longed for the giant's sweet meat, so he returned to the forest. Death was not pleased at being bothered so much, but he told the boy to go into an inner room in his house and help himself. The young man was horrified when he picked up a bone and recognized it as belonging to his sister, and when he looked round he saw that all the meat was from his sister and her servant. The village people crept into the forest, and were afraid at the sight of the giant. Then they planned to set light to his long hair, which stretched far all around. They watched from a safe distance and saw the giant tossing and sweating as the flames approached, and at last they reached his head and he lay as dead. When they got near the young man saw in the roots of the giant's hair a packet of magical medicine. He took it out and showed it to the people. An old man suggested that they might try to sprinkle some of the powder on the bones in the giant's hut. When this was done the missing girls and boy sprang up alive again. The young man suggested putting some of the magical powder on the giant, but the people protested for fear he might come back to life. The boy put just a little powder on the eye of Death. It opened at once, and everybody ran away in fear. It is from that time that Death has come among men. Every time the giant opens and shuts his eye somebody dies.

Jackal, Snake and Masks

The Dogon stories say that the jackal who had seized the fibre skirt of his mother Earth had committed incest, and the skirt was reddened with

Left: the Luba of Congo produce fine miniatures like this wooden headrest of a male and female figure facing each other, with fan-like hair styles and bead decorations. Man and woman as the basic unit of human life often appear together in African art and mythology, sometimes as twins, and show their dependence on one another. British Museum.

A wooden stool carved by the Luba of Zambia. The legs are shortened to give importance to the head and body, the latter being decorated with abstract designs that many women have tattooed on their bodies as marks of beauty.

blood. It was put out to dry on the primeval ant-hill, and later was stolen by a woman who put it on and reigned as queen. This spread terror around and eventually men took the skirt from the woman, dressed in it themselves as kings, and forbade women to wear it. But the oldest man had not been told of the theft of the skirt, and this breach of respect to him brought its own penalty. When the old man died and was changed into a Nummo spirit, he did not go up to heaven at once, but continued living on earth in the shape of a great snake. One day some young men had put on fibre skirts and were entering the village when the snake stopped them. He rebuked them furiously, speaking in their own mortal language. But this was a further breach of order, for as a spirit he should have used the spirit language. By speaking the human language he cut himself off the spirit world, he could go neither to heaven nor to earth, and he died. So death came to men.

The snake lay dead on the path to the village, and the young men fled in horror to tell their elders. They all came back and resolved to take the corpse to a cave, wrapped in the fibres which had caused its death. But the soul of the dead man was looking for somewhere to go, and it entered the womb of a woman in the village. When her child was born he was red like the fibre skirt and spotted like the snake. He became normal in adolescence, when he was dedicated to the vanished ancestor. In this ceremony a log of wood, in the shape of the snake, was painted in its colours, and sacrifice was offered to the spiritual principles of the dead reptile. From that time arrangements had to be made to provide places and ceremonies for all who died, and people were chosen for their proper

Wooden figure of a bull from Malagasy A story says that God set the bull on guard outside the house where the remedy for death was kept. The bull was so thirsty that he drank some of the remedy, and when God came the snake accused the bull of theft. Since then men sacrifice the bull to save themselves from death—but the bull is immortal.

maintenance. From this arose art, particularly the carving of wood. Wooden images represented dead people, and wooden masks represented animals that men killed. Rules and taboos were formed to see that both individuals and groups paid proper respect to the dead.

An ancestor figure from the Ivory Coast, seated on a stool representing a leopard and with a cockerel—probably one was used in propitiatory rites—at his feet. Carved wood.

Struggles with Death

A myth from Togo tells of the river god Tano fighting with Death. Long ago there was a hunter in the forest who for a long time failed to catch anything. After many days he saw and hit an antelope, but it bounded away and a long chase followed. The man went after it but when it went into a cave the creature suddenly turned into the god Tano. The man was terrified but Tano told him not to fear, for he would protect him in the future. The two set off for the man's home and on their way they met Death. Death challenged them, and Tano replied that he was going to live with man. Death said he would not allow this, and sang a chant of defiance at Tano. Tano replied defying Death, and for a whole month the two great beings sang against each other. Death could not force Tano back along his path, but neither could Tano compel Death to let him continue on the road to man's home. Finally they agreed on a compromise. When a man fell ill, whichever of the two spirits reached him first would have power over him. If Tano arrived first the man would get better, but if Death got to his bed first the man would die. So Tano did get to man's abode, but Death came too.

A story from the Mbundu of Angola tells of two brothers one of whom, Ngunza, had a dream while he was away from home that his brother had died. When he got back he demanded who had killed his brother, and his mother said it was Death. He vowed to fight Death, and got a blacksmith to make a great iron trap.

He set this in the bush, watched it with great vigilance, and successfully caught Death. Death pleaded with Ngunza to let him go, but he refused, saying that Death was always killing people. Death denied this, alleging that people died by their own fault or that of somebody else, and if Ngunza would release him he could visit his land and see for himself. Ngunza consented and four days later they set off for the family of the dead. Death told him to watch the new arrivals, and of each one he asked what had killed them. Some said it was their own vanity, others jealous husbands, and so on. They had all died through the fault of some human being, and so it was unfair to blame Death.

This fits in with the general belief in Africa that death is never natural, but always due to the malice of some person. Death told Ngunza that he could go and search for his brother, and he was happy to find him living much as he had done on earth. Ngunza said that they should go back to their earthly home, and he was very surprised that his brother did not want to go, for he was much happier where he was (see the Chaga story of the radiant sons in heaven, page 63). Ngunza had to return home alone, though Death gave him the seeds of all the plants that are cultivated in Angola now; an addition that explains the origin of agriculture.

A further part of the story says that Death came to look for Ngunza himself at his home, and pursued him from place to place. Finally Ngunza protested at this treatment, saying that he had done no harm, and it was Death himself who said that he did not kill anyone. But the only answer of Death was to throw his axe at Ngunza, who turned into a spirit.

The World Beyond

The last story has told of the land of death, and the myth of Kintu spoke of the heavenly country. Many other myths tell of journeys to the world beyond death, either below ground or up in heaven. The Mbundu of Angola also speak of a king Kitamba whose head wife died. The king was so grieved that he went into perpetual mourning and insisted that all his subjects should do the same. People were forbidden to make noise, or speak in public. The village chiefs protested, but the king refused to change his order unless his wife was restored to him.

The elders in despair consulted a famous doctor and he agreed to help. He had a grave dug in his house and entered it with his little boy. He instructed his wife to dress in mourning but to make sure that the grave was watered every day. The grave was filled in and the doctor and his boy set out for the underworld. They came to a village where they found the dead queen, and she asked them where they came from. The doctor told her of her husband's excessive grief, and the queen pointed to a man nearby and asked if he knew him. When the doctor said he did not, the queen said it was Death, who was consuming them all. Then she pointed to another man, who was chained up, and asked the doctor if he could recognize him. The doctor was surprised to see that the man looked like king Kitamba, and the queen said that in a few years he would die. She affirmed that once a person died he could not return, but she gave the doctor an armlet in proof that he had been to the land of the dead.

Meanwhile the doctor's wife had been pouring water on she grave every day and eventually the earth began to crack. As the looked her husband's head began to appear from the ground, and he came out pulling his son with him. The boy fainted in the sunlight, but with the help of medicines his father restored him. He reported to the village chiefs and received his reward. They gave the news to the king, who recognized the armlet and gave orders for mourning to cease.

In a story told by the Chaga of Kenya a girl, Marwe, and her brother were sent by their parents to watch a field and keep monkeys away from the beans. They sat on guard all day, but in the afternoon they were so hot that they crept off to a distant pool for a drink. When they got back the monkeys had stripped the field bare. The children were so afraid of the anger of their parents that Marwe threw herself into the pool. Her brother rushed off to take the news home and the parents were so distressed that they forgot to be angry. However it was too late, for Marwe had disappeared. She sank down through the water till she came to a hut where an old woman lived with her children. The old woman took care of Marwe, who worked for her and shared the life of the underworld. After a long time she became homesick and asked permission to leave. The old woman did not object, but asked her whether she would like the hot or the cold. The question was mysterious, but a choice of goods is common in such stories.

Marwe chose the cold, which should have been disagreeable, but when she dipped her arms into a cold pot she drew them out covered with rich bangles, and she put in her feet and legs with the same result. The old woman gave her a fine bead petticoat, told her that her husband would be called Sawoye, and sent her home. Marwe rose up to the surface of the pool and sat on the bank. News soon spread that a beautiful and rich girl was there. All the country went out to see her and many wanted to marry her, from the chief down. But Marwe refused all till Sawoye came along. He had an offensive skin disease and people marvelled at the choice, but it was cured as soon as they were married. With Marwe's bangles they bought many cattle, but this aroused the jealousy of the neighbours and Sawoye was killed. However Marwe brought him back to life with her magic and hid him inside their house. When the enemies came to divide their spoil Sawoye came out and killed them. Then the couple lived happily ever after.

Another Chaga story tells of a girl who one day went out with her friends to cut grass. She saw a place where it was growing luxuriantly, but when she put her foot there she sank at once into the mud. Her friends tried to catch hold of her hands but she sanker deeper into the mud and disappeared, singing out that the ghosts had taken her and her parents should be told. The girls ran home and called all the people to the quagmire. Here a diviner advised that a cow and a sheep must be sacrificed. When this was done the girl's voice was heard again, but eventually it faded away and was silent. However on the spot where the girl had gone a tree began to grow, which got taller and taller till it reached the sky. It was a useful tree under which boys would drive their cattle in the heat of the day. One day two boys climbed up the tree, calling to their companions that they were going to the world above. They never returned. The tree was called the Story-tree.

The Ronga of Mozambique tell of a girl who broke her pot on the way to draw water. In great distress she cried out for a rope, and looking up she saw one hanging from a cloud, like the ropes in the stories of God leaving the earth. Climbing up she found a ruined village in the sky and an old woman sitting there asked what she wanted. The girl told her story and the old woman told her to continue walking, and if an ant crawled up into her ear she must leave it alone. The girl did so, and coming to a new village heard the ant whisper to her to sit down. As she sat at the gate some elders came out in shining clothes and asked what she was doing there. The girl said she had come to look for a baby, (a new theme in the story which is perhaps mixed with another).

The elders took her to a house, gave her a basket, and told her to collect some corn from the garden. The ant whispered that she should only pull one cob at a time, and arrange them carefully in the basket. The elders were pleased with her work, and with the cooking that she did on the ant's instructions. Next morning they showed her some babies on the ground, wrapped in red and white clothes. She was going to choose the one in red clothes, when the ant told her to choose white. This she did, and the old men gave her the baby, and as many cloths and beads as she could carry. Then she found her way back to her family and they were overjoyed at her treasures and her baby. Perhaps she had been barren before; babies are often said to be prepared in heaven and their parents designated for them.

An additional narrative says that the girl's sister was jealous and set off for the heavenly land to seek the same good fortune. She got up to the sky, but she was a rude and wilful creature, who refused to listen to the old woman or heed the warnings of the ant. When she saw the babies she chose a red one, there was a great explosion and she fell down dead. Her bones dropped on her home, and people commented that heaven was angry with her because she had a wicked heart.

Left: the Ijaw people of the Niger delta carve wooden figures to represent spirit companions, the medium through which they converse with ancestral spirits. The figure is said to tremble when requests for help and guidance are heard.

Figure of a woman from the Zulu of South Africa. A Zulu myth says that the first man and woman came out of a reed which suddenly exploded. A similar story is told by the Thonga of Mozambique, and it used to be the custom to put a reed in the ground outside a house in which a baby was born.

Gods and Spirits

After the Supreme Being there are many other spirits in which people believe. Some of them may be called personifications of natural forces and others glorified heroes of the past; some are both. Groups of gods are worshipped in West Africa, and some other parts of the continent, though often they are vague powers with little mythology. Stories of some of the more important spirits will now be told. But first it may be asked why men pay attention to many spirits, and not one God alone. One answer may be that people cannot afford to neglect any power that can influence their lives, just as they do not pay attention to one person alone but to the many officials with whom they must deal. Another reason is suggested in a story told by the Mende of Sierra Leone.

At first men did not pray, but they came to the Supreme Being with small complaints. God considered how he could make men know his will. He created a mountain and gave it the ability to talk to men, thinking that if men were used to the voice of the mountain, and kept its laws, they would also hear the divine voice and laws. He also gave men the power of dreaming.

One night an old man had a dream in which he saw the mountain coming to him as an old man and calling him friend, saying that he must tell the village chief to get his people to bring food for the mountain to eat. The dreamer asked where the old man had come from and he answered that he came from the mountain. The dreamer looked towards the mountain and saw that it had disappeared, and the old man said that was because he was the mountain. After the old man had gone away the mountain could be seen again. When the old man awoke he told the chief about his dream. All the people were assembled, the story was told, and it was agreed to give food to the mountain. But they told the old man to ask the mountain for help to catch the animal that would be needed for food. So he went with his sons, picking up twenty stones on the way.

At the foot of the mountain he cleared a space and called out to the mountain that if it really did need food it must arrange the stones so that it could be known how many animals were needed. The dreamer and his sons went home, but next morning they came back and found the stones set out in order. Nine stones faced the mountain, and that meant that nine animals would escape. Ten stones were facing the man and so ten would be killed. One stone was in the middle and that animal must be kept alive till sacrificed by the dreamer. This was done when the men went hunting. Then the village men collected rice, salt and palm-oil from their women and took them with the meat to the mountain. The women were sent back because there was not enough food for them. The live animal was sacrificed, and meat, rice and oil were put on leaves. The dreamer took a kola nut, which splits into halves and is a sign of friendship. He called on the mountain to show whether the food had been received and appreciated, and tossing the halves of the kola nut into the air he let them fall to the ground. They fell with their white side facing upwards, a sign of acceptance. This was done four times, and the sign of acceptance always appeared.

The dreamer asked the mountain to protect the town against warfare, save women in childbirth, protect children against witchcraft, heal all who were sick, and care for the people as they had cared for the mountain. Every year the mountain was a place of prayer for men, and they brought gifts to it. But God had pity on the women who were not allowed to share in the sacrifice. He told a woman in a dream to pray at a great rock, and since then men and women have prayed at mountains and rocks, and also at trees and rivers.

Sun and Moon

There is not much mythology of the sun and moon, for in tropical Africa the sun is always present and there is no need to call it back in the winter as men did in the cold countries of northern Europe or Japan. Occasionally some of the gods are connected with sun and moon, like Mawu and Lisa of Dahomey (see page 21). Mawu as the moon is more kindly and so beloved of men, while Lisa the sun is fierce and harsh. Mawu is older, woman and mother, gentle and refreshing. During the day men suffer under the sun's heat, but in the brilliant cool moonlight they tell stories and dance. Coolness is a sign of wisdom and age, so Mawu is the wisdom of the world, and Lisa its strength. Sometimes Nyame, God of the Ashanti, is personified as the moon and represented by the queen mother, whereas another personification of the truly Great Nyame, Nyankopon, is in the sun and the king.

The Bushmen and Hottentots of South Africa tell stories of the sun and moon, which suggest that they paid more attention to these heavenly bodies than the negroes did. A Hottentot story links the coming of death with the rising and waning of the moon, rather than with God as in much negro story, though the theme of the messengers is the same. The moon once sent a louse to assure men that as the moon died and lived again so would they. On its journey the louse met the hare and told his message. The hare said he could run faster and would take the message. But when he arrived he told men that as the moon dies and comes to an end so men would die and come to an end. The hare told the moon what he had said and the moon was angry at the distortion of its message to men. He seized a piece of wood and hit the hare on the lip. Ever since then the hare has had a cleft lip, and its flesh is taboo.

The Cape Bushmen tell a similar story, and also a variant in which a young hare was weeping at his mother's death. The moon appeared and told him not to cry, for his mother was not dead but only asleep and that she would come back alive, just as the moon dies but returns. But the hare did not believe him and kept on crying, saying that the moon was deceiving him. The moon was angry, and cursed the hare and cleft his lip.

Some of the Pygmies say that it was the moon who created the first man and put him on earth. His body was moulded, covered with skin, and blood poured inside. Then the moon whispered to him that he should give birth to children who would live in the forest. The story goes on to say that the Pygmy was told that he could eat of all the trees in the forest, except of a taboo tree; but he broke this commandment and that is why death came to men. But, like some other Pygmy stories, this one may have been influenced by negro or Christian story. However it is told by some Pygmies today. The pygmy myth has already been told of the Moon instructing the Lightning in the mysteries of birth.

The Krachi people of Togo say that the sun married the moon, and

Left: door panel of the Yoruba, elaborately carved with the motifs which recur frequently in the art and mythology of the people. Serpent, lizards, and twins can be seen. British Museum.

Wooden carving of a follower of Shango, storm god of the Yoruba of Nigeria. The marks on the cheek indicate the clan. The double-bladed axe on the head is the symbol of Shango who is said to throw his axe, the thunderbolt, when there is a storm. Shango was fourth king of the Yoruba and so fierce that he had to retire to the forest. Some say that he hanged himself, others that he ascended to heaven and rules from there. British Museum.

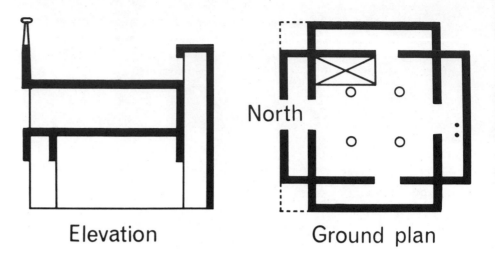

Elevation   Ground plan

the two gave birth to the many stars. But as time went on the moon got tired of her husband and took a lover. The sun was angry and would not have his wife with him in the house any longer. However, he divided his possessions with her, and some of the children stayed with him while others went away with the moon. But the moon remains dissatisfied, and she goes into her husband's fields. The children that stayed with the sun then fight the moon and her stars, and that is the cause of storms. However the moon does not like the children to fight too long, and sends a messenger to pacify them by waving a cloth of many colours, the rainbow. Sometimes the sun himself catches the moon in his fields, and he tries to sieze and eat her. That is why when men see an eclipse beginning they shout and beat drums so as to frighten the sun into letting the moon go.

The Dagomba of Togo say that the sun has a marketplace, which can be seen when a halo appears round the sun. Here he keeps a ram, and when it stamps its feet that causes thunder, and when it shakes its tail

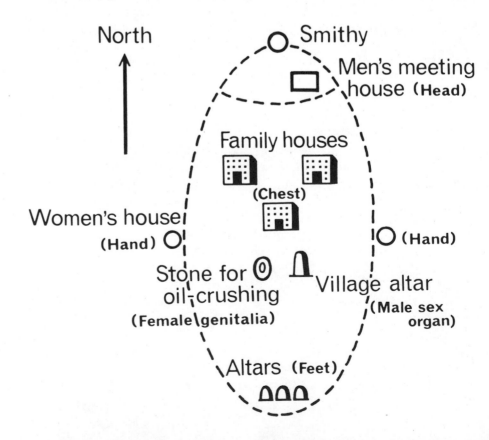

Left: the shape of the Dogon house is symbolical. The floor is like the earth and the flat roof like heaven. The vestibule is a man and the central room a woman, with store rooms at her side as arms. The hearth at the end is her head. The four posts are the man and woman entwined in union. So the family house represents the unity of man and woman, and God and the Earth. From Griaule: *Conversations with Ogotemmêli.*

Left, below: like the house the Dogon village represents human beings. The smithy is at the head like a hearth in a house. The family houses are in the

centre and millstones and village altar represent the sexes. Other altars are at the feet. From Griaule: *Conversations with Ogotemmêli.*

Far left: mask of the Kob water-antelope, called Horse of the Bush, by the Dogon of Mali. The dancer who wears it has an arrow in his hand and a horsetail, and he puffs and throws dust while dancing.

Right: wooden statuette of the Dogon of Mali, called the Figure Which Stands on the Terrace. Normally kept in a house, it is brought out for the funerals of rich families.

that is the lightning. The rain is the hair falling off the ram's tail and the wind comes from the ram rushing round and round the market. The marks on the face of the moon are given fanciful explanations. Some say they are an old woman sitting on a stool in the moon, others that they are an old man beating a drum, and yet others that they are a man on horseback with a spear in his hand.

A story told in Angola says that the son of the first man refused to marry a wife from his own people and declared that he would only have the daughter of Sun and Moon. He tried to find a messenger to take his proposal up to heaven, but animals and birds refused. At last the frog said he would carry the message. The frog had found that girls came down from heaven on spider's webs to draw water, so he hid himself by the well, jumped in one of their jars, and was carried up to the sky. There the frog gave the message to the Sun, and the Sun said he would agree to the marriage if the youth came himself bringing the first present of the dowry. The frog went back with the news, the youth asked the price, and the frog told him it was a sack of money. The young man collected this and sent the frog up to the sky with it, but he refused to go to heaven himself, for the frog must bring the girl down. The frog reached the sky and hid himself in the girl's room that night. While she was asleep he stole both her eyes. In the morning the Sun and Moon discovered this and asked a diviner the cause. The diviner said her suitor had cast a spell on her and if she were not sent to him the girl would die. So the sun ordered the spider to weave a big cobweb and take his daughter to earth. The frog went on in advance and told the young man that his bride was coming. When the girl came down the spider's web, the frog gave her back her eyes and took her to her husband's house. They were married, and the wife went up to heaven no more. Only the frog retained this power, and it is said that frogs sometimes fall from the sky in rainstorms.

An unusual story told by the Chaga of Kenya suggests that the Moon-Chief and his followers were more backward than people on earth. A boy, Murile, was being chided by his mother and so he took his father's stool and invested it with magic. He told the stool to go up in the air and it obeyed, carrying him first of all into a tree and then after more incantations right up into the sky. There the boy looked round until he found some people, and asked them the way to the village of the Moon-chief. They made him work for them for a time and then sent him forward with directions. The same thing happened with other groups that he met; he worked for them, and then was sent on, and finally he arrived at the Moon-chief's village. There he was surprised to see people eating

Wooden twin images from Dahomey, joined by seven links, all from one piece of wood without joints. The male twin smokes a pipe. Twin images are used in rituals to ensure the health of the twins, and if they die the mother carries the images in her skirt band.

Right: Ikenga (personal shrines) are found in almost every house in the province of Onitsha in Nigeria. As the token of a man's life force, they are customarily destroyed on the death of the owner.

Snakes are common in African art, and especially the non-poisonous python which is often held to be sacred. Painted wooden carving from Cameroun. Museum für Völkerkunde, Munich.

raw food, and when he saluted the Moon-chief he asked why they did not use fire. He was told that they did not know about fire. So he offered to show them, and was promised many cattle and sheep in return. Then with two pieces of wood and dry grass he lit a fire, and was hailed as a great magician.

Murile became rich, with wives and children, flocks and herds. But after many years he wanted to return home and sent messengers to announce his coming. The mocking-bird went and sang that Murile was coming back, but the family would not believe it, thinking him dead, and drove the bird away. Murile too would not believe that the mocking-bird had been to his home, so the bird went again, seized his father's stick in its beak, and brought it back as proof. Murile then set off, with

all his family and herds. But the way was long and tiring, he could not go straight back on his magic stool because he had to take his herds down the slope where heaven joins earth. Murile was tired, but a great bull in his herd promised to carry him if he would vow never to eat its flesh. Murile agreed and arrived home in triumph. His family were overjoyed to see him and he settled down in peace. He made his parents promise never to touch the bull, but when it was very old his father killed it and his mother took some of the fat and put it in Murile's food. As soon as he tasted it the meat spoke, reproaching him for breaking his promise. Murile began to sink into the ground, and as he called out to his mother that she had deceived him he disappeared from sight, and that was the end.

Another story of the struggle of the Sun and Moon, comparable with the Togo myth, is told by the Luyia of Kenya. God created the Moon first and then the Sun. In the beginning the Moon was bigger and brighter, and the envious Sun attacked his elder brother. They wrestled till the Sun was thrown down and pleaded for mercy. Then they wrestled again and the Moon was thrown in the mud and dirt splashed over him so that he was not so bright. God intervened to stop them fighting again, saying that the Sun would be brighter henceforth and shine during the day for kings and workers. The Moon would only shine at night, for thieves and witches. It is said that the Moon was foolish in showing mercy to the Sun and should have beaten him thoroughly the first time. But it often happens in mythology that the younger brother takes the leading place, as in the story of Jacob and Esau.

When God had made Sun and Moon he made two big stars to shine in the east and west. He made a great red cock who lives in the clouds and sends lightning when it shakes its wings and thunder when it crows.

A Luyia myth tells of another visit to heaven, this time to the Sun. A girl who was being pressed to marry a man she did not like ran away into the bush. After going about twelve miles she came to a rope hanging down from the sky. When she took hold of it she was lifted up to heaven and put down on a rubbish heap outside a village as the day came to an end. As she sat there the mother of the Sun came along and asked who the girl was. She said she was a new arrival, and the Sun's mother said the girl could stay with her, but her son was chief and would want to marry her. The girl agreed to go with her but said she could not marry a chief. The Sun's mother encouraged her and took her home, saying her son was in the garden, and if the girl saw something red and bright she must not cry. When the Sun returned everything looked brilliant as lightning, and the girl laid down to cover her face. The Sun's wives told him that his mother had brought a new wife and he went to salute her. But the girl cast her eyes down and did not answer. Then the Sun sent his chief servant, the Moon, to speak to the girl, but still she did not reply. Six servants were sent in turn, but were all unsuccessful. The servants said they had been wrong in not taking presents to the girl, so the Sun sent her something of all that grew in the land, but still the girl would not speak. Finally the Sun decided to give her his own rays and took them to the girl himself. At last she replied, in a thin voice, and all the servants brought oil to anoint her as bride. They were married and she bore the Sun three boys.

But all this time the rays of the Sun were in a pot which he had given his wife as a present, and they did not shine on earth. So the wife asked for permission to visit her parents on earth and some servants to carry presents to them. The Sun agreed and dropped a rope to earth down

which they all climbed with presents. The girl's parents were astonished to see her, for they thought she was dead or lost in the bush. They brought a black ox to kill for a rite of purification before they could salute her, but she refused it. They brought oxen of other colours, but she shook her head. Only when they brought a white ox did she accept it, and it was sacrificed, and its flesh given to the people who had come from heaven. After three days the girl and her servants set out to go back to heaven, and when they seized hold of the rope they were drawn up so quickly that she had no time to say farewell to her parents. The rays of the sun had not shone yet, but when they reached the Sun's house his wife opened the pots where the rays were and they began to shine on earth. This brought joy to mankind, and the Sun told his wife that his chief servant, the Moon, would shine at night.

Storm Spirits

More important for ritual in many places are the spirits of the storm, for tropical tornadoes not only bring the expected rains but often cause damage with thunderbolts and flashes of lightning. Remarkable stories are told of Shango, the storm deity of the Yoruba of Nigeria. This divinity was once a man, it is clearly said, and lived as the fourth king of that people, ruling over a kingdom stretching into neighbouring countries. Shango was a strong ruler, and a great doctor, but also tyrannical. He could kill people by breathing fire from his mouth. Eventually his tyranny was challenged by two ministers, and to avoid their attack he set them to fight against each other hoping that both would be killed. One was slain, but the victor turned on Shango himself who fled to the forest. He went on horseback, taking his three wives and some loyal followers. But after wandering about for a long time only his favourite wife remained loyal, and finally in despair Shango hanged himself from a tree at a place called Koso.

This shameful end of the terrible king caused a great stir. When travellers brought reports that the monarch had hanged himself, his enemies mocked those who were still faithful to him. So his friends went to a great magician to find out how to bring fire on their enemies' houses. Some say they could make fire descend from heaven, others that they threw small gourds filled with gunpowder on to roofs during storms. Anyway there were many fires, and the followers of Shango said this proved that the king did 'not hang' (*ko-so*). Shango was showing his anger by sending fire from heaven and sacrifices must be made to appease him. This was done and a temple built at a place still called Koso, (*ko-so*), to contradict the story that Shango hanged himself. The version of the myth given by priests is that Shango was angry with his discontented subjects, so he disappeared into the forest on a horse. When a search party went after him they only found the horse, and a voice came from the sky saying that Shango did not hang, but ascended to heaven by a chain and would rule from there by thunder.

The Yoruba compare the noise of thunder with the bellowing of a ram, and these animals are sacred to Shango and wander freely about marketplaces. Thunderbolts are called 'thunder axes' and are said to fall to the ground whenever there is a storm. Priests of the storm and their acolytes often carry symbolical 'thunder-axes', with wooden handles and finely decorated thin metal blades. Sometimes these axes are double-headed, like those found in parts of the Mediterranean world.

A girl's wooden doll from Ashanti, Ghana. Almost abstract, the round high head represents a mark of beauty. Women also carry such dolls in the back of their skirts to ensure that their children are well formed.

Right: past and future, death and life, are illustrated in this skin-covered helmet-mask from the Ikoi of Nigeria, which represents dead—yet living—members of the Ekpo society. Like Roman figures of Janus the head has two faces looking in different directions. The male is black with closed eyes like the past, and the female is light with open eyes looking to the future. Survival after death is firmly believed in, the idea of 'total' death being unacceptable to the African mind.

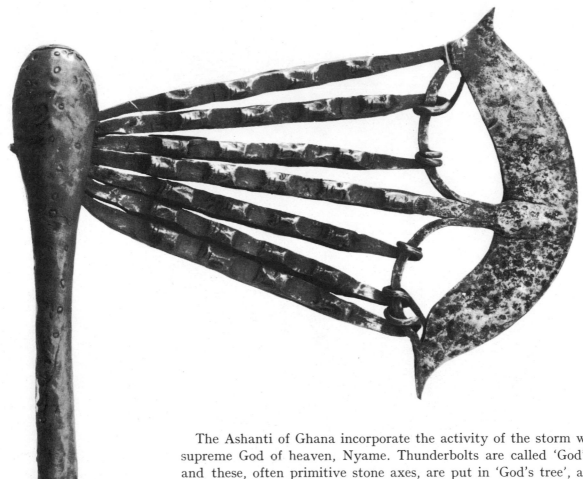

Ceremonial axe from the Songye-Bushongo, Congo. Such axes are carried in many African countries in rites of gods and ancestors. The handle is copper and the wrought iron blade decorated with fifty-eight heads on the two sides. Horniman Museum.

Right: gold badges from Ashanti, Ghana, worn by the royal soul-washers or soul-bearers, whose task it was to keep the soul of the king free from danger and contamination from evil. The abstract designs are finely worked in the metal that gave Ghana its old name of the Gold Coast. British Museum.

The Ashanti of Ghana incorporate the activity of the storm with the supreme God of heaven, Nyame. Thunderbolts are called 'God's axes' and these, often primitive stone axes, are put in 'God's tree', a forked post standing by doorways containing a pot with simple offerings.

The Fon of Dahomey say that when the Creator had made all things, he retired and divided the universe among his children. The Earth was the elder and having quarrelled with the Storm decided to go below, taking all his inheritance. The Creator agreed, and said that the brothers must be like the two halves of a calabash, Storm above and Earth below, and they must not fight. But trouble came when the Storm stopped rain falling. Earth was king below, and people complained that they were dying of thirst under his rule. Finally Earth had recourse to the Oracle to find out why no rain had fallen for three years. The Oracle said that the Storm was angry because Earth had taken all their father's inheritance. Then Earth remembered that he had stuffed all his property into sacks, but there was no room for fire and water and he had left them behind. On the advice of the Oracle he made a sacrifice of his possessions and sent a bird to report this deed to the Storm. The Storm was appeased, saying that though Earth had taken everything he himself had been able to get all these goods simply by controlling fire and water. As a sign of reconciliation he gave a great clap of thunder and heavy rain began to fall. Since then the brothers have been reconciled and rain falls each year, while the bird that took the message is sacred to priests of Earth.

A story of the Songhay of the upper Niger says that one of the celestial spirits, Dongo, had an axe and flew up to the sky to try it out. He arrived over a village with his companions. One of them made a spark, and Dongo threw his axe. There was a flash of lightning and some men below were killed. Dongo was surprised at this and went off to ask his mother how he could repair the damage. She took him to his grandfather, who gave him an earthenware pot full of water. Dongo plunged his head into the pot and filled his mouth. Then he sprayed it over the dead men, and they all came back to life. Dongo said they had been killed because nobody in the village had sung his praises, but he taught them a prayer-spell which would avert harm from the storm in future.

In southern Africa it is widely held that lightning is a bird, and some people claim to have seen it. It is variously described as a great brown bird, or a fish-eagle with a white neck, or with red legs and shining feathers like a peacock. The bird is said to lay a big egg where it strikes, and some think these bring good fortune while others say they are unlucky and must be destroyed by a doctor. If the lightning bird itself can be caught it is of great value for medicine. People who are struck by lightning are said to have been scratched by the claws of the bird.

In the Congo region it is said that lightning is a magic dog which gives a sharp bark. A story says that a man found a beautiful dog and took it home. As it was raining he took it into his house and lit a fire to dry the dog. There was a great explosion and man and dog vanished for ever. Sometimes the lightning is called a great chief who goes hunting with twenty-four dogs which are the lightning flashes. Stories are told of men caught up to heaven by the lightning, but allowed by God to return to their earthly families.

One of the most popular spirits worshipped by the Hottentots was a great hero and rain god Tsui'goab. The myth says that he went to war with a chief called Gaunab, sometimes identified with death, because he killed many people. Gaunab kept overpowering the hero, but the latter grew stronger after each battle, and finally he destroyed Gaunab by smiting him a great blow behind the ear. But as Gaunab was dying he made a last effort and hit his enemy on the knee. Ever since then the conqueror has been called Tsui'goab, meaning 'wounded knee'. He was a great chief and magician. He made the first man and woman, or some say the rocks out of which they emerged. Although he died several times yet he came back and there was great feasting. Tsui'goab is worshipped as giver of rain, living in the clouds, and invoked with the first rays of dawn. He is called Father of Our Fathers, and implored to send the streaming thunder-cloud and nourish flocks and men. He gives health, and men take oaths in his name, showing that he is regarded as a moral deity. Some writers have taken him to be the Supreme Being, but recent opinion sees him as a hero and rain deity, an ancestor who came from the east, and a father who gives rain and cattle.

Other spirits have the storm as one of their functions. The Dinka of the Sudan believe in Deng, who is an important god but rather difficult to define. Some say he was the ancestor of all the Dinka people. He is closely connected with thunder and lightning and his name is used for the rain. The lightning is Deng's Club, and people struck down by it are not given proper mourning. Both rain and human birth are manifestations of Deng, and in some myths he is the son of heaven and earth.

Kibuka, the Buganda war god, has storm characteristics. He was brother of the great god Mukasa and when a king of Buganda sent to ask for divine help in war, Kibuka was sent to give aid. He was warned to be wary of the enemy and never let them know his battle stations, or have any dealings with their women. Kibuka flew up into a cloud and hovered over the enemy, shooting down arrows and spears on them, while the human army fought successfully below. So Buganda won the first battle and took some women prisoners. One of these took Kibuka's

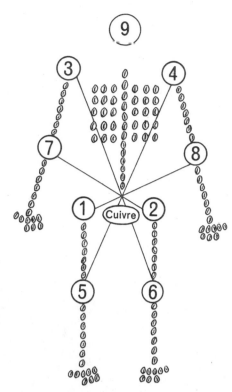

Dogon symbol of a human body as an ancestor called Lebé, which is the outline of every soul which the Nummo spirits make at birth. It is made of different coloured stones, according to the eight ancestors, with an extra stone for the head. The spirits put copper between the legs as the metal which was later used for ritual bracelets. The stones symbolize the life-force of the eight ancestors which is transmitted to their descendants. From Griaule: *Conversations with Ogotemmêli.*

Below: sketch of a Dogon ancestral temple. It is a cube about nine feet high at each side, with towers in front and an iron symbol like lightning above the door. The walls are painted with pictures of snakes, birds and abstract patterns. The platform at the right of the door is for priests to sit on during ceremonies, and to the left are meal-grinding stones. Inside are altars of earth, thunderstones, pots and iron or wooden tools. From Griaule: *Conversations with Ogotemmêli.*

fancy and he carried her off to his hut. But after discovering who Kibuka was and where he posted himself in battle, the woman escaped and told her people all about it. When the battle was resumed Kibuka started hurling down his weapons and the enemy archers sent a volley into the clouds which mortally wounded him. He flew off to a tall tree and died there, and the king of Buganda was killed with many of his people, so that there was no king for some time.

Kibuka's body was found in the tree and taken down for burial. A temple was built for him, enclosing his jawbone, as was done for Buganda kings. Priests were appointed to serve him and in time of war some of them accompanied the army to give messages from Kibuka.

Rainmakers and Rainbows

Those who make rain fall and those who make rain cease are found all over Africa. Often they are wise men who observe the signs of the times and the secrets of nature. They are prophets, like Elijah, who can tell whether small clouds in the distance will bring rain. A Luyia story from Kenya says that in the beginning nobody could predict or control the rain, until there was an old woman who had lost her family and wandered about everywhere; she encountered many peoples during her travels and gained the knowledge of how to control the rain. She began to show her powers, but when rain fell there came also thunder and lightning, and snakes and crawling things came into houses. So people were afraid and expelled her from their midst. Eventually the woman went to live with a man to whom she revealed the art of making rain fall. As his powers became known people went to ask the man for rain, but he told them that it was not free and they must bring him presents for his work.

An additional story says that the rainmaker was told to demand higher prices after a time, since he was like a chief and spent his time looking at heaven and earth. He should not be content with small gifts of tobacco, but should demand goats and cows. The people brought him goats, but not until there was a long drought did they fear they had not given him enough, so they fattened cows and paid these large fees in time of great need. Since then there have been many people who have known the art of rain-making. The story of one of the most famous, the Rain-queen of the Lovedu, is told later.

The rainbow is regarded not so much as beautiful but as strange and dangerous, though it is also attractive in the sense that it has magic powers. The Luyia say that God created rain and all the water on earth came from it. To stop the rain from falling when it was not needed, God made two rainbows. The male rainbow is narrow and the female is wide. The male cannot prevent rain by itself, but if it appears first and is followed by the female rainbow, then the rain stops.

The double rainbow also appears in Fon mythology in Dahomey. It is a symbol of the snake, the red part being the male portion of the snake and the blue the female portion. The snake, which supports the earth (see page 22) is often found in double form in art and story, and it is believed that one snake is twined round the lower earth and another appears in the sky. The fantasy of treasure to be found 'where the rainbow ends' is widespread. The treasure may be the bright Aggrey beads which are popular for decoration. Or it is gold which is dug out of mountains and called the snake's riches.

In southern Africa it is said that if a man finds the place where the rainbow ends he should run away as fast as possible or he will be killed. Some people say it is unlucky to point at a rainbow, for if you do your finger will become stiff. But the Ila people of Zambia point at the rainbow with a pestle to drive it away. They think that where the rainbow ends there is a fierce ram which burns like fire.

The Zulu of South Africa call the rainbow the Queen's Arch, one of the frames which form the house of the queen of heaven. Some people call it a sheep, or a being who lives with sheep. But the Kikuyu of Kenya say it is an evil animal which comes out at night to eat men and animals. The Masai of Kenya say there was such a being that lived in Lake Naivasha, where the flamingoes gather, and it swallowed their cattle, till at last the young warriors managed to kill it.

A Chaga story of Kenya tells of a man who was looking for God to ask him for some cattle. He found the end of the rainbow and stood there offering his prayer. He did this many times but no cattle came. So in anger he cut the rainbow in half with his spear. Half the rainbow flew up to the sky, and the other half made a deep hole in the ground. The man disappeared, but some other people came along and found the hole. They climbed down to the underworld and found a rich country, with many cattle, and to prove their words they brought back bowls full of milk. But when other people went down they found lions there and fled back emptyhanded. This resembles other stories, of two kinds of people visiting the underworld or heaven.

Other natural phenomena have tales told about them. One day a young man of the Songhay of the upper Niger regions was walking in the scrubland near the bush on his way to market. He saw a whirlwind, a dust-devil, coming straight towards him. In fear he threw his spear at it, and the wind passed him by, but when it had gone he could not find his spear any more. This surprised him, but in time he forgot about it. Then one day as the youth was walking through a market he saw a man who had a spear just like the one he had lost. He went up to him and demanded where he had found the spear. The man smiled at him, for he was the spirit of the whirlwind. He simply asked the youth if he did not remember the whirlwind that had blocked his path one day when he was going to that very market.

Earth Spirits

Belief in a spiritual power animating the earth is almost universal and is found all over Africa. Usually, though not always, the earth is thought of as female, and sometimes as the wife or partner of the heavenly God. Sometimes they are in opposition, or there is conflict between the earth and another celestial deity, and this appears in some of the myths already given.

The Ashanti of Ghana speak of Earth Thursday (Asase Yaa), because Thursday is sacred to the earth. There is no temple of this deity, but work on the land is taboo on Thursday. In the spring farmers offer a sacrifice of a fowl before digging the soil, praying for permission to dig, protection against accidents, and a fruitful harvest. The earth is also concerned with the dead, and before a grave is dug a libation is poured and permission asked. The earth is knocked, a custom that has survived among the descendants of the African slaves in America.

One of the most important earth goddesses in Africa is Ala of the

Female ancestral figure of the Dogon of the western Sudan. The aloof face and highly stylized body indicate the power of the ancestors.

77

Wooden carving of a warrior and horse from a Dogon ancestral sanctuary in Mali, representing the Guardian of the World.

Ibo people of eastern Nigeria. Ala is ruler of men, source of morality, and protector of the harvest. As a mother she gives fertility to the crops, and also to human beings. As queen of the underworld she receives the dead into her pocket or womb. The cult of Ala is shown vividly in sculptures which show the attitude of the people to divinity and to life in general. Shrines to Ala are found all over Ibo country, but in the southern regions of Owerri special houses, called Mbari, are erected. These are only built for particular occasions and are not temples, and once built they are abandoned and new ones erected. The Earth Goddess is always to be seen as the central figure in a group of mud sculpture. Mbari houses are built at the order of priests of Ala, when they say the goddess has sent a sign, such as the appearance of a nest of bees, or a snake, in the priest's garden. Men and women are chosen to do the work, and they live together in chastity for weeks or months.

The Mbari houses are square, with open verandas round a closed central chamber. They are filled with mud figures, brightly painted. In the middle, facing the road, is Ala, Mother of Earth. She usually has a child on her knees, holds a sword in her hand, and her legs are often painted in spirals like the brass rings that girls used to wear at puberty. Facing Ala is the Storm God, a subordinate counterpart of the goddess. Then there are sculptures of Ala's family, the water goddess, and other deities, and with all manner of clay figures of gods, men and animals, and all kinds of occupations, old and new. There are figures of Africans and Europeans, dancing girls and district officers, hunters and policemen, tailors at sewing machines and women giving birth to babies. There are many animals: elephants and snakes, dogs and monkeys, forest creatures and monsters. All the gamut of life is there, without any distinction of sacred and secular. Some of the sculptures are sexual, some tender and pathetic. Ala and her child in some scenes recall the Italian Madonna and Child. Christian symbols are included in the old pantheon.

Earth spirits include those of rocks and hills. Great mountains, like Mount Kenya, Kilimanjaro, and Mount Cameroon are all regarded with reverence and stories are told about their powers and taboos. A king of Buganda who wanted to build on the sacred hill of Boa crossed the stream at the bottom and at once became blind. The blindness remained as long as he stayed on the hill, but left him immediately after. There was a sacred forest there which only a priest could enter, and a temple with a female medium. If the chief of the district allowed the path round the hill to fall into disrepair, or a grass fire caught any of the trees, the medium would threaten him with an illness of burning sores. A story of Mount Kenya will be told later.

Other earth spirits belong to the forest and are patrons of hunters. The Songhay of the upper Niger, though superficially Moslems, believe in a spirit called Musa (perhaps from the Arabic for Moses) who is a great traveller, hunting everywhere, and he surveys the four cardinal points of the compass. Having learnt everything that there was on earth by his travels, he taught men the secrets of hunting, and also of pottery and weaving. Musa had seen his mother take clay and by means of water turn it into pots as hard as iron. He saw the wild tortoise weaving and he told men how to weave strands of cotton together. He knew the ways of the forest, and showed men the twelve trees whose bark could be crushed into powder and mingled with water, and the resultant mixture would make a man who washed with it invisible to the animals of the forest.

The gods of iron are often connected with hunting. The Yoruba of Nigeria say that Ogun, the god of iron, used to come down from heaven by a spider's web and hunt in the marshes, in the olden days when the earth was a watery waste. Later, the earth was formed by Great God, who set about arranging everything in order. But he came to thick forest that his tools could not cut, since they were only bronze. Ogun alone, whose axe was iron, was able to clear a way, and he only did this after the other gods had promised to reward him. So when they built their sacred city of Ilé-Ifé, they gave him a crown. But the iron god did not want to rule his fellows, since he still enjoyed hunting and battle, and for a long time he lived alone on a hilltop, from whence he could watch over the land and spy out his prey. When finally he came to the gods they did not want to harbour him, for his clothes were stained with blood. So he made clothes from the bark of a palm tree and went to live elsewhere.

A myth told by the Fon of Dahomey says that the great deity Mawu sent his child Lisa to earth with a metal sword (in other stories Lisa is the male consort of Mawu, see page 21). Lisa came down to clear the forests and show men the use of metal, so that they could make tools for ploughing the fields and cut down wood for houses. Lisa told men that without metal they could not survive and so he re-created the order of the world which at first had been without metal. Lisa then returned to heaven and Mawu gave him the sun as his domain. A metal sword is called Gu (the Yoruba Ogun) and this is the Dahomean name for the god of metal to this day. He is protector of warriors, hunters

A bronze figure of Ol-okun, sea god of Benin, Nigeria. With royal coral dress and mudfish legs, he holds lizards in both hands. God of water and wealth, he lives in a palace under the sea with human and fish attendants, and sometimes sends floods on earth.

Far left: a carved and painted figure of the Dogon of Mali, used in rain-making. The open hand calls down the rain, the closed one stops it. The figure wears a lip-plug and the prominent navel is a common sight due to bad midwifery. The Dogon do not know the origin of these ancient figures, which are kept in granaries and receive offerings.

Left: the Mossi of Upper Volta use this antelope mask both at funerals and to protect the fruits of the earth. The lower face of the mask is abstract, but on it stands the Earth Goddess with a lively figure and bright painted eyes.

Right: male ancestor figure of the Fang of Gabon, masters of the sculptured form. Made in carved and polished wood, it was mounted on a cylindrical box which held the bones of the ancestor. British Museum.

Far left: painted clay sculptures of the Ibo, Nigeria. The central female figure is the great Earth Mother, Ala. Next to her is a European, wearing a sun helmet and riding a motor cycle.

Left: Ibo temple in eastern Nigeria. The walls are painted with figures, the man on the left being encircled by a snake. Skulls from sacrifices hang from the lintel, and a fence of the sacred dracena shrub surrounds the temple.

Overleaf, left: the interior of a famous temple of Shango, god of storms, at Ibadan, Nigeria. The posts are carved with mythical figures of gods and men, and the priest sits among other carvings. Behind him is an altar bearing the thunderstones which are said to fall from the sky during a storm. The spots are for decoration, though old temples of the smallpox god were also dotted in this way.

Overleaf, right: to the Maconde people of Mozambique the Mapico mask represents evil spirits which are driven out of the village by drumming. Human witches and sorcerers are greatly feared and where possible ostracised.

and blacksmiths, oaths are sworn on his symbols, and nowadays he is also claimed as guardian of motor lorries and bicycles, which carry bunches of feathers blessed by his priests.

Water Spirits

All the great waters, and many lesser ones, are believed to be inhabited by powerful beings. The Owner of the Sea, Ol-Okun, is believed by the Yoruba and Benin peoples of Nigeria to live in an underwater palace with a great retinue, the attendants being both human and fishlike. In clay and bronze sculptures the majesty of the Owner of the Sea is illustrated, and stories say that he tried to rival the splendour of the Creator himself. Olokun challenged God to appear in his finest dress and he would do the same, and the winner would be declared by public acclaim.

On the day chosen God sent his messenger, the chameleon, to fetch Olokun. But when the latter emerged from his ocean palace he was astonished to find that the messenger of God was wearing a splendid dress similar to his own. He turned back quickly, and put on even finer robes and more coral beads, but when he came out the chameleon had also changed into the same dress. Seven times Olokun tried to outdo the divine messenger, but each time he was matched by the same costume. Finally he gave up the struggle, thinking that if God's messenger was so glorious God himself must be much greater. Ever since then Olokun has taken second place to the supreme Deity, even though people pay him more attention in ritual. The myth may reflect ancient stories of the struggle of the sea and the land, or of a primeval flood after which

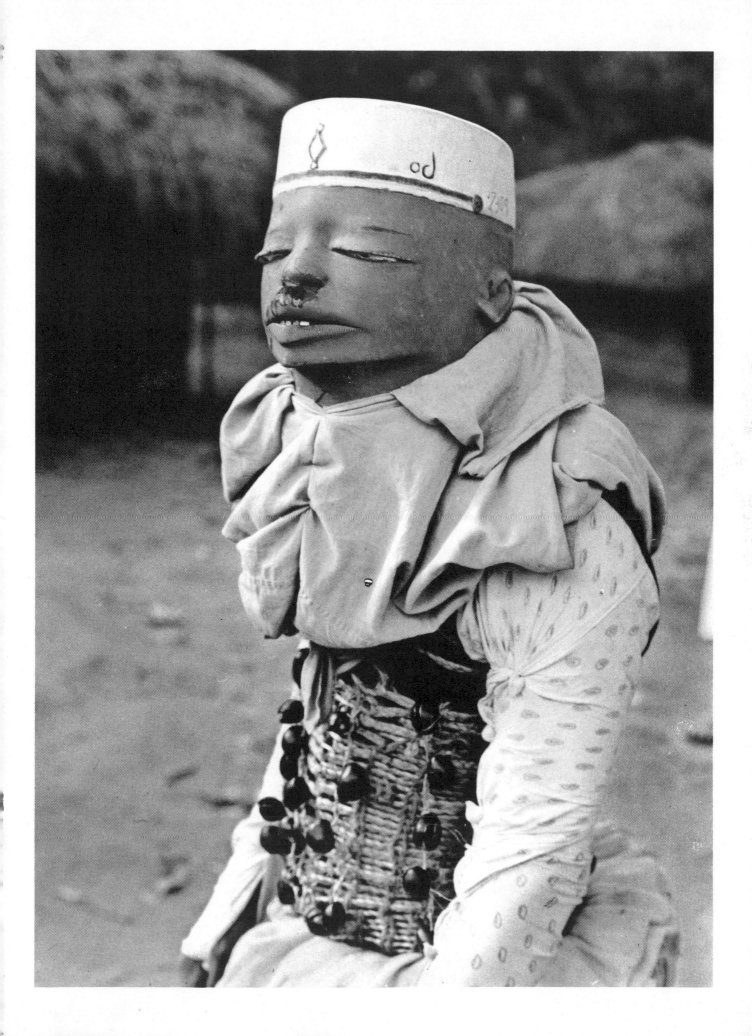

the sea was kept within proper bounds.

In Ghana and the Ivory Coast the river Tano is one of the most important deities and is credited with creation, as son of the supreme God. A story was told earlier of his struggles with death, and he was rival also of the river Bia, who was eldest son of God while Tano was the second son. Bia was the obedient child while Tano was often wilful, so when the children came to manhood God decided to give Bia the fertile places and Tano the barren areas. God called the goat, told him what he proposed, and said he must call the boys so that each could take his lot. But the goat was a friend of Tano and told him to be sure to get to God's house early in the morning, disguised as Bia, so as to receive the best portion. Then the goat went on to Bia, gave the message, but said there was no hurry as God was busy. So Tano dressed in his finest clothes and went early to God, deceived him, and received the fertile land. Later Bia came along and God discovered the mistake, but the portion had been given and could not be changed, so Bia had the barren land. The story again resembles that of Jacob and Esau.

Lakes too are believed to be inhabited by spirits and a remarkable example is Lake Bosomtwe in Ghana. Like the Dead Sea this lake has no outlet and the water evaporates in the heat. A story says that long ago there lived an old woman who was a leper and so had no husband or children. One day there came a god out of the lake called Twe. When he tried to make love to the old woman she protested, saying that she lived by herself and if she bore a child she would not be able to get food and water. Twe said that when she wanted anything she had only to knock on the lake and fish would come. So they were united, and she bore a son called Twe Adodo, son of the lake god, and founder of a clan which claims the lake spirit as protector. Once a week Twe would come out of the lake with his followers, and every year his son would go into the lake and ask his father's help with fishing. Then the lake would 'explode its gunpowder'. This exploding of the lake happens irregularly, when the vegetable matter gathered in the bottom decomposes and the accumulated gases cause loud noises and make horrible smells. The fishermen are forbidden to use iron hooks or nets in fishing, since the lake spirit is thought to dislike them, and they paddle with their hands on logs or rafts.

The Songhay of the upper Niger tell many stories of water spirits called Zin (perhaps from the jinn or genie of Islam). There was a lake belonging to a snake who was a Zin, and one day when the snake was taking the air it saw a woman and wanted to marry her. The parents agreed but as dowry they demanded ownership of the lake. The snake gave it to them and went to live with his wife some distance away, where they had a family. From time to time the snake returned to his house at the bottom of the lake, from where he controlled the fish, crocodiles and hippopotami. When the snake died his place was taken by his son, who is still guardian of the lake. But he is not pleased with men who have entered the lake with iron weapons, and because of that the hippopotami left the lake.

Another Songhay story says that once a village chief went out fishing by himself at night, and he was astonished to see, in the middle of the river, a sort of round hut. When he drew near he saw a little sheep in the midst of the waters. The chief was afraid and began to recite magic spells. But while he gazed the sheep changed itself into a little baby, and he knew it must be the great snake of the river that had transformed itself. The chief crouched down in the bottom of his canoe and began

Wooden ram's head from Benin, Nigeria. It is pierced at the back and fitted on a staff when in ritual use.

to shout for help. His brothers in the village heard him and came to his assistance, but when they got there he was dead, for he had seen a Zin, and that is forbidden to mortals.

A favourite story of the Songhay and of many peoples of the Niger bend, tells of a great struggle between a man, Faran, and a river spirit called Zin-kibaru. This spirit had gained great power by magical charms and musical instruments, and ruled over the fishes and animals of the river. Faran had rice fields and every night Zin-kibaru came and played his guitar there and all the fish came and ate Faran's rice. One day Faran went fishing and only caught two hippopotami. He was ashamed to see his mother cook this tiny meal, and calling his assistant he went off in a canoe to fight Zin-kibaru. They met on an island where seven streams crossed; Zin playing his guitar and others drums and violins and dancing. Faran demanded the guitar and Zin-kibaru said they should fight for it, but if he won he would take Faran's canoe. Faran was small and fat, and Zin-kibaru tall and thin. But Faran was winning when his opponent uttered a spell; 'The palm leaf despises the hippo.' Faran fell and lost his canoe. So Faran went back to his mother in shame and weeping. But his mother said he was stupid, for to fight a spell one must use another and she taught him one. Then Faran took a larger canoe and set off for Zin-kibaru. They met and fought, and the Zin fled. Faran pursued him, they fought again, and the Zin fled once more. A third time they fought, and as Faran was winning, Zin-kibaru said, 'The palm leaf despises the hippo.' But Faran retorted, 'If the sun strikes it, what happens to the palm leaf?' Then Zin-kibaru fell to the ground and his musicians all jumped into the river leaving their instruments behind. Faran seized the guitar, Zin-kibaru's harpoon, and all his slaves, and took them home in triumph. So the human hero conquered the Zin or dragon, set free other spirits who were subject to him, and gained his musical instruments and weapons.

Most of the Buganda rivers were said to have originated from human or divine beings. Two rivers sprang forth from the son and daughter of King Tembo, who married each other. One of the rivers was said to have been caused by the birth-flood, and later it was worshipped under the form of a leopard because, it was said, a leopard was drowned in it. Another river came from a young woman who was travelling about looking for a lover who had embraced her and then deserted her. On the spot where her child was born a river sprang forth. On each side of the river there was a heap of grass and sticks, and everybody who wanted to cross would throw sticks on the heap as offering to the river spirit, and after a safe transit a thank offering was thrown on the other side.

Some Malagasy clans, whose name means 'son of crocodile', have a myth to explain this. One says that the mother of the clan used to live in a river with a crocodile as husband. One day she was caught in a trap and married a man, but after bearing him two sons she returned to the river. Since that day her descendants hold the crocodiles as taboo and are never hurt by them. Another story says that when a member of the clan dies an old man drives a long nail into the forehead of the corpse so that it cannot move. But when it is put in the family grave a few days later, the nail is taken away and the body told it can move as much as it likes so as to return to the royal abode where the ancestors are waiting. When the grave is closed the corpse moves a little, a long tail grows behind, the hands and feet change into small limbs with claws, and the skin becomes hard and scaly. Finally it becomes a crocodile, and goes off to the river. The family sacrifice a bull to it once a year.

A dancer's headdress worn in fishing rites by the middle Niger river. The wooden figure decorated with metal represents Faran, the master of the river. He struggled with Zin-kibaru, a river spirit, who had magical charms and musical instruments. Zin defeated Faran at first with spells, but Faran's mother taught him a stronger spell and he overcame Zin, captured his guitar, harpoon, and all his slaves, and so ruled the Niger.

87

Oracles and Divination

There are many kinds of oracles, by which men try to discover the future or the unknown past, or the will of God and the ancestors. There was no writing in tropical Africa in the olden days, but there were complicated systems of divination which used notation that was a kind of writing or means of recording and communicating. Such systems are known from Senegal to Malagasy, but the most famous is the Ifa divination of the Yoruba of Nigeria, which has been borrowed by neighbouring countries. Ifa is a spirit often identified with a god called Orun-mi-la, 'heaven knows salvation'. In some versions it was he who directed creation under the orders of God. When God had all the elements of creation ready, he sent the morning star to call the gods, but only Orunmila came. The morning star told him that the materials of existence were kept in a snail shell which was in the Bag of Existence, lying between the thighs of God. Orunmila took this, came down below, scattered soil and got a hen and a pigeon to spread it abroad, as in the other Yoruba creation myths (see page 20).

Another story says that after living on earth for some time Orunmila went back to heaven, stretching out a rope and climbing it. But since he had been interpreting the will of God to men, they now found themselves helpless and without guidance. Then Olokun, the Owner of the Sea, came and destroyed most of the earth and it became unfit for habitation. So in pity Orunmila came down again and made it pleasant.

The Yoruba say that under the name of Ifa, a man-god, the oracle came from heaven and was born of superhuman parents who had never been to earth. He was sent by God to put the world right: give help in sickness and childbearing, teach the use of medicine, and give guidance on secret or unknown matters. Ifa came down, stopping at various towns on the way, setting up centres for consultation, but he was not satisfied till he got to the sacred city of Ilé-Ifé where he established his home, and this is still the centre of his worship. Ifa was a great linguist, knowing all the tongues of earth and heaven, and he can advise men of every nation and bring messages from the gods. He was a great doctor, and songs and proverbs used in his worship speak of his powers. The Ifa divination is performed by casting nuts in combinations of four and sixteen, and marking a pattern on a divining board.

The Fon of Dahomey, who have borrowed the Yoruba system of divination, have their own stories of the origins of the cult. They call it Fa, and say that after the creation of the world two men came down from heaven. In those days there were very few people on earth, no gods were worshipped and there was no medicine. So these divine messengers called men together and told them that God had said every man must have his own Fa. When people asked what the Fa was the men replied that it was the writing which God creates with each person, and by this they could find out what tutelary god to worship and how to do the will of God. The heavenly messengers selected a man, whom they taught how to work the oracle. They had brought from heaven some nuts of a special palm tree, which could be manipulated so as to reveal the messages of Fa. They showed the man how to throw the nuts

from one hand to the other, trace patterns on a board according to the number of nuts left over from the throw, and so discover his destiny. They told him to gather up the sand which bore the resulting pattern, inscribe it on a piece of calabash, put it in a small cloth bag, and so keep the secret of his horoscope. Since that time divination has been performed on this pattern, both for ordinary occasions and to make a life horoscope.

This is the most complicated system of divination, though simpler methods of using strings with objects attached, and judging the oracle by the patterns made when they are thrown on the ground, are found in many places. In the Transvaal the Venda people use four pieces of flat ivory for divination, and other peoples use dice of wood carved with designs of beasts like crocodiles. The four dice represent members of the family: old man, young man, old woman, and young woman. They are thrown into sixteen possible combinations and diviners have interpretations for each combination.

Divining bowls, filled with water and an assembly of objects, are used for discovering secrets or detecting witches in parts of tropical Africa. But in southern Africa apparently only the Venda and the Karanga of Rhodesia use such divining bowls, with patterns and pictures round the side of the bowl, and a cowrie shell in the middle which is called the umbilicus and represents the spirits of the mother. However in the ruined buildings of Zimbabwe in Rhodesia similar soapstone bowls have been found, decorated with figures such as bulls.

A famous oracle was at Aro in eastern Nigeria, and during the time of the slave trade he was widely feared and called by Europeans the Long Juju. The oracles were given from a cave seven feet up the bank of a little river. Visitors stood in the river, while the priest was in or by the cave, and gave answers in a nasal voice, like the oracle at Delphi. People who were guilty of crimes, or declared to be so, were said to be 'eaten' by the oracle, and they passed through the cave or some other route to be sold into slavery. This trade was destroyed in 1900, though the oracle is still respected.

The greatest of the demi-gods of Buganda, Mukasa, was a great giver of oracles, a kindly deity who never asked for human sacrifice. Myths say that when Mukasa was a child he refused to eat ordinary food and disappeared from home, later being found on an island sitting under a large tree. A man who saw him there took him to a garden and lifted him on to a rock. People were afraid to take him into their houses, thinking he was a spirit, so they built a hut for him on the rock. They did not know what to give him to eat, for he refused all their food, but when they killed an ox he asked for its blood, liver and heart. Then people

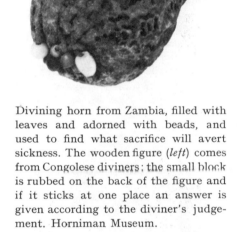

Divining horn from Zambia, filled with leaves and adorned with beads, and used to find what sacrifice will avert sickness. The wooden figure (*left*) comes from Congolese diviners; the small block is rubbed on the back of the figure and if it sticks at one place an answer is given according to the diviner's judgement. Horniman Museum.

Left: ivory divining rod from the Yoruba of Nigeria, used in worship and fortune-telling. The designs are usually in pairs, male and female, representing spirits, and some rods have little clappers at the end to invoke them. The diviner takes the heavy end in his hand and strikes the divining board with the pointed end, murmuring prayers and chants inviting the spirits to be present and hear the prayers. In the possession of the author.

Divination board or planchette of the Yoruba, Nigeria, with figures of gods and animals round the side. Powder or sand is sprinkled in the middle and the diviner marks patterns on it with his fingers. British Museum.

Old ivory divining tablets of the Bushmen of the Kalahari desert, Botswana. The diviner beat the leather strips joining the tablets with his hand and invoked the oracle to tell the truth. Then the tablets were jerked from his hand and the direction and person at which they pointed gave the answer required.

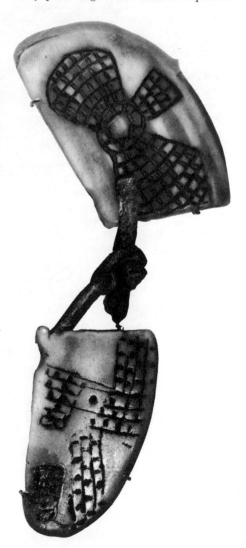

knew he was a god and consulted him in any trouble. Mukasa lived on the island for many years, married three wives, was cared for by priests, and at last disappeared as suddenly as he had come.

His temple was a conical reed hut, which was rebuilt at intervals on the express orders of the king. Originally it is said that Mukasa spoke his will directly to the priests, but later they used mediums who uttered his messages. The medium never entered the temple but had a special hut in front of it. When seeking to know the will of Mukasa she smoked some tobacco until the spirit came upon her, and then she announced in a shrill voice what was to be done. The medium was not allowed to marry, or walk about in the sight of men, or talk to any man but the priest, and once chosen held the office till death.

Connected with the oracles are often other messengers who act as intermediaries, between the gods and men. The Yoruba of Nigeria have many images of an intermediary spirit called Eshu, who is both a messenger and a guardian of man. His image is placed outside houses and villages. But he has an unpredictable character, and is often violent or crafty, and he may express the anger of the gods at human wrongdoing. Eshu is very powerful and only the Supreme Deity can curb his might. One day the Storm God was boasting that he could subdue every other spirit. Eshu asked if that statement included him. The Storm God at once apologized and said he did not count him in this category. Another god bought a slave without consulting Eshu, and when he found his slave strangled next morning he knew who was responsible.

A popular story tells how Eshu introduced discord into the house of a man with two wives with whom he lived at peace. Eshu did not like this, as he delights in confusion, and he laid a trap. Changing himself into a trader, he made a beautiful headdress and stood in the marketplace. One of the wives came down, saw the fine hat, and bought it. She showed it to her husband and he favoured her in such a way that the other wife was jealous. She in turn went to the market, and found Eshu there with a hat far better than the first. She took it home and became her husband's favourite. Then the first wife went again, and the same thing happened; the second went later, and so on. The rivalry grew in intensity, with the husband's affections swaying first to one side and then to the other, till nobody knew where they were. Then Eshu left off going to market, the women were in despair, and the family was engulfed in strife.

The Fon of Dahomey have similar beliefs about a kindred spirit called Legba. In the beginning Legba lived on earth with God and only acted on his orders. Sometimes God told Legba to do something harmful and then people blamed Legba for it and came to hate him. They never gave him credit for his good deeds but thanked God instead. Legba got tired of this and went to ask God why he should always be blamed, since he was only doing the divine will. God replied that the ruler of a kingdom ought to be thanked for good things and his servants blamed for evil.

Now God had a garden in which fine yams were growing, and Legba told him that thieves were planning to plunder it. Therefore God called all men together and warned them that whoever stole his yams would be killed. During the night Legba crept into God's house and stole his sandals, put them on and went into the garden. He took away all the yams. It had rained not long before and the footprints were clearly seen. In the morning Legba reported the theft, saying that it would be easy to find the thief from the prints. All the people were called but nobody's feet fitted the prints since they were too big. Then Legba suggested that perhaps God had taken the yams in his sleep. God denied this and accused Legba of his usual mischief, but when he consented to put his foot down it matched the prints exactly. The people cried out that God had stolen from himself, but God replied that his son had tricked him. So God left the world, and told Legba to come to the sky every night to give an account of what went on below.

A variant, giving another version of the stories of God retiring to heaven, says that when God and Legba lived near the earth Legba was always being reprimanded for his mischief. He did not like this and persuaded an old woman to throw her dirty water into the sky after washing. God was annoyed at the water being constantly thrown into his face and he gradually moved away to his present distance. But Legba was left behind and that is why he has a shrine in every house and village, to report on human doings to God.

Legba is closely associated in Fon story and ritual with the oracle Fa. One myth says that Fa had sixteen eyes, the nuts of divination. He lived on a palm tree in the sky. From this height Fa could see all that went on in the world. Every morning Legba climbed the palm tree to open Fa's eyes. Fa did not wish to convey his wishes by speaking out loud, so he put one palm nut in Legba's hand if he wanted two eyes open, and two palm nuts to have one eye open. Then he looked round to see what was happening. And so today one palm nut thrown by the diviner is a sign for two marks to be made on the divining board, and two nuts make one mark.

Later God gave Fa the keys to the doors of the future, for the future is a house of sixteen doors. If men used the palm nuts correctly they opened the eyes of Fa and showed the right door of the future. Legba worked with Fa, and when there was a great war on earth which threatened to destroy everything God sent Legba to teach the method of the Fa divination, so that men could consult the oracle and know the proper way of conduct.

The Yoruba made beautiful vessels to hold the seeds used in divination. This bowl is held in the hands of a characteristic Yoruba carving of a mother carrying a child.

Witches and Monsters

Mask of the Mpongwe of Congo (Brazzaville), made of wood with the face painted white with kaolin to represent a female ancestor, with impassive features, decorated forehead, and elaborate hair style.

Right: picture cloth from Dahomey, with appliqué patterns representing rituals for expelling evil spirits. The snake arches over all. Figures on the left carry gongs to frighten evil away, and those on the top and bottom right have symbolical axes showing rams' heads with lightning coming from their mouths, emblems of the storm god, Shango. The devil in the top centre is of European design, as shown by wings and tail.

Witchcraft is believed in throughout Africa. Basically it is the belief that certain people, chiefly women, have the power of changing themselves into other forms, when they prey on the bodies and souls of their enemies or even their relatives. It must be firmly said that it is a delusion. People do not leave their bodies or destroy the souls of others. So in fact there are no witches, though many people believe in them. Witchdoctors try to treat and cure those who are thought to be bewitched. Many African peoples distinguish witchcraft from magic and sorcery. Magic is the practice of making charms to help or harm people, so the good magician, medicine-man or doctor, is a respected figure. But the bad magician or sorcerer is hated and works in secret.

A Hausa story of Nigeria tells of a man who had three wives, all of whom had magical powers but only two were witches. They used to dance in the forest, and the two tried to persuade the third wife to do a witchcraft dance with them. She put them off by saying that the dance was too difficult and they must wait until she had given her husband a gift of cloth. Then she warned her husband of what was afoot and he pretended to go on a journey, but really he was rolled up in his mat and stayed quiet. When they thought he was gone the wives began to dance. The two witches chanted that they would offer up their husband to the witchcraft dance; one said she would have his liver and the other his heart. Then the husband jumped up, beating one wife and driving her out, and tying the other to the top of a tree. Then he lived in peace with the faithful one.

Another Hausa story tells of a witch who had nine mouths on her body, but of course they could not be seen. One day she went to get leaves from a forest tree and boiled them as broth for her husband and his father. When the husband opened the bowl of soup it cried out in warning, 'Cover me up, for if you do not you will die.' Then the husband's father uncovered his broth and it also cried out, 'Cover me up, for if you do not you will die.' So the husband got his own soup and his father's and threw both bowls over his wife's head. At once her nine mouths became visible, she was shown as a real witch, and she ran away.

Apparently circumstantial stories are told of people who have left their bodies at night and flown off on bats or owls to cannibalistic feasts in the tree tops. In the Ivory Coast a witch is said to have changed into an owl, though her body was still asleep on the bed. The owl flew out but was shot by a brave hunter, and at the same moment the witch died in bed. Another story says that a witch changed into a crocodile, and while a girl was bathing the crocodile seized her and dragged her into the water. But a man killed the reptile with an axe and at once the witch died in the house where her body had been lying. It was the witch's soul that went off in an animal body, and in many stories it is not the victim's flesh that is thought to be eaten by witches but 'the soul of the flesh'.

The forest, bush, plains or any lonely places are thought to be the lair of dangerous spirits. There are 'half-men' who have only one hand, leg, eye and ear. A Gikuyu story of Kenya tells of such a being whose

A wooden dish of the Ibo people from the Brass River region of southern Nigeria. Such dishes were used when offerings of food were made to the gods.

Right: house post of the Bangwa people of Cameroun. A remarkable piece of carving from a single trunk, it stands ten feet high. The four figures represent ancestors. Museum für Völkerkunde, Munich.

body was half flesh and half stone. Elsewhere such men are said to be half human, half wax. In Malawi such a being is supposed to have haunted the forests, challenging anyone to wrestle with him, and offering medicines to a man strong enough to hold him down. Then there are 'little people', perhaps early pygmies, though later regarded rather as fairies. Some lived on the highest mountains, like Kilimanjaro, which formerly were beyond the reach of human feet. Elsewhere there were mischievous imps, who could help or harm human beings.

In a Swahili story a girl found a beautiful shell on the seashore, and put it on a rock while she went on with her companions to look for more. Then she forgot it till they were nearly home, and asked her friends to go back with her. They refused and she had to go alone, in the dangerous dusk, so she sang to keep her courage up. On the rock she found a fairy, and when he heard her he asked her to come closer and sing the song again. Then he seized the girl and stuffed her into a barrel. He went along from village to village, offering to play wonderful music in exchange for a good meal. When the fairy beat the barrel like a drum the girl sang inside and people gave him plenty of food, but he gave none to the girl.

In time he reached the girl's own village. They had already heard of his fame and begged him to give them an entertainment. When the girl sang her parents recognized her voice, so they gave the fairy a great deal of wine afterwards to make him fall asleep. They rescued the girl, and put bees and soldier ants into the barrel, so that when the fairy next beat it he would be severely stung.

In southern Africa there are Xosa and Lesotho versions of this story, in which the parents put poisonous snakes into the barrel and the fairy dies. In another version he throws himself into a pool to get away from the snakes and a pumpkin tree grows on the spot. Later some boys take one of the large pumpkins home, but their elders are horrified, knowing what it is, and chop it to pieces.

Then there are dangerous animals that may take human form for a time, like the 'were-wolves' of ancient Europe, though there are no wolves in tropical Africa but dangerous beasts like lions and hyenas. A story told with variants in Kenya, Zambia and Malawi, and no doubt elsewhere, tells of an obstinate girl who would never marry any of the suitors who came to her. Her parents were so angry that they offered to give her to anybody who presented himself. One day there was a great dance to which men came from other villages. A very tall and handsome youth arrived with a ring round his head like a halo. All eyes were drawn to him and the girl followed him all the time. The dancing continued for days, the girl danced with the beautiful young man a great deal, and fell in love with him.

But her brother happened to see that the fine youth had a second mouth at the back of his head, and warned his mother of danger. She ridiculed the idea that such a handsome man was evil, and when he demanded their daughter's hand both parents agreed with joy. The wedding was celebrated and some days later the girl and her husband set off for his home. But her brother followed at a distance, still feeling uneasy. As they got farther away the husband asked his wife if she could still see the smoke from her parent's house, and she said she could. Later he asked if she could see the hills behind her home, and she could just discern them. When they had at last disappeared the animal in human form told his wife to weep her last tears for he was going to eat her. But just then the brother shot at him with a poisoned arrow, saved his sister, and took her home.

In similar stories the younger brother accompanies the sister and husband, and at night the husband goes out and changes into animal form, as a lion or a hyena. Having prowled around he tries to break into the house with other lions to devour the two humans. But the brother has strengthened the thorn-bush defences and they are safe for a time. When the animal in human form returns, the brother makes a drum, or a miniature boat, and by his magic makes it rise in the air. He and his sister cling to it and thus escape.

There are many tales about monsters which swallow human beings and then are killed by a hero. In a Zulu tale there lived in a mythical river a great bearded, humpbacked monster. One day the daughter of a chief went to bathe in the river with her companions, against the warnings of her parents. When the girls came out of the river they found that all their clothes had been taken, and each girl politely asked the monster to give them back. All succeeded, except the chief's daughter, who refused to plead with the monster and was seized and dragged into the river. When the chief heard the news he sent his young warriors to attack the beast and rescue his daughter, but they too were swallowed up. Then the monster went to the chief's village and devoured all the people, even eating the dogs and cattle.

The father of two beautiful twins escaped, however, and he swore revenge. He took his club and spear and went after the beast, who had disappeared. First he came across some buffaloes, who told him which way to go. Then he met some leopards, who directed him forward. Next he came to an elephant, who also sent him on. At last he met the monster, and she apparently hoped to deceive him, for she told him to stay on the same path and proceed. But the man was not fooled, he demanded his children, and stabbed the monster in her great hump. The wound was fatal and she died. Then all the people, the cattle and the dogs, came out of her mouth, and last of all the chief's daughter who was restored to her father. In another version it is the girl herself who kills the monster and sets the people free, and in similar tales a herd-boy or young hero makes the beast so uncomfortable that she pleads to be cut open and all the victims are released.

Ghosts, particularly those of people who have not been properly buried, are believed to dwell in the bush and to trouble unwary travellers. Animals and trees have souls as well as men and may have ghosts. A story told by the Dagomba of Togo says that a chief long ago wanted to show his people that he was greater than anybody else. So he called them all together and said that in future he would no longer ride a horse but a dappled antelope. His hunters were sent into the forest to catch such an animal, and after a long time they succeeded. But they did not know that their dappled antelope was a ghost. When the chief ordered his men to saddle the creature they encountered great difficulty, though they managed in the end. Then the chief leapt into the saddle, but the antelope at once dashed into the forest, with the chief clinging to its back.

The hunters pursued him as fast as they could, but both antelope and chief were lost from sight and have never been seen again. So it is said that whenever a chief from that town is about to die, people see a dappled antelope come in the night and stand outside the chief's house waiting to take him away.

Secret Societies and Ancestors

A Bambara 'standing' mask from Mali. These strange constructions, of carved wood decorated with cowrie shells, were used in the initiation rites of the Ndomo society.

Right: ebony figure of a doctor from Mozambique. The doctor may be a medicine-man who knows the secrets of nature and tends the sick, or a witch-doctor trying to cure those who are thought to be bewitched. Most gods of sky, earth and water have priests who perform sacrifices in their temples, and the doctor may be a priest as well. He is a wise man and much respected.

In many parts of Africa there are closed associations which are popularly called secret societies. They serve various purposes, of which the initiation of young people and the representation of dead ancestors are the most common. The masquerades of their officials, 'masked spirits', in fantastic dress, are some of the most striking and most photographed of all African religious ceremonials. The mythology of the secret societies is not easy to obtain, since they are secret except to initiates. The great number of such societies would demand volumes to record even part of them. So as an example one of the best known is chosen here, the Poro, of the Mende people of Sierra Leone.

The Poro, meaning perhaps 'no end', can be traced back for several hundred years and is related to other West African societies. Various myths account for its origin. One says that long ago there was a rich old man who had a large family, and so much land that he was looked upon as the chief of that place. But trouble came to him and he was struck with a disease of the nose, so that his voice became very harsh. The people had never seen such a disease before and they were afraid. They isolated the old man in the forest outside their village. Only his chief wife and youngest daughter were allowed to look after him, and when elders went to discuss business with the chief they went alone. Everyone else was forbidden to approach or to attempt to look on him. Eventually the men plotted to kill the chief and his wife and daughter, in order to seize his lands. He was already out of sight and all that could be heard was his harsh voice, so they planned to make an instrument that would imitate it. This was done by making a hollow stick, with a piece of skin fitted over one end. Then the village people were told that the chief had become a spirit. Occasionally it was said that he was coming to the village to visit the rest of his family. A herald came announcing this and all the women and children were rushed out of sight into their houses. Then the herald called out that the chief needed rice, goats, and so on, and these were provided.

Another version says that the first chief of this people was very powerful, and when he died the elders were afraid that the whole community would break up if his death became known. So they kept it a secret and found a man who could imitate his voice. As the late chief had a strongly nasal tone it was easily copied. The first person to act as imitator was bound by oaths of secrecy, and when in due time others had to be told, they were bound to secrecy also.

More rational explanations, though not more likely, are given of the origin of the Poro society. One is that it came from groups of people hiding in the forest from slave-raiders and bound to mutual loyalty. Another suggests that it arose from chiefs holding meetings in the bush to avoid being overheard by women, or away from the spies of their enemies in wartime. Yet another suggests that very sick people were isolated in the bush, and even after their death their voices were heard, being copied by instruments made to frighten women and children into submission. The story says that the elders acquired all the man's property, but when his children grew up they were introduced to their father,

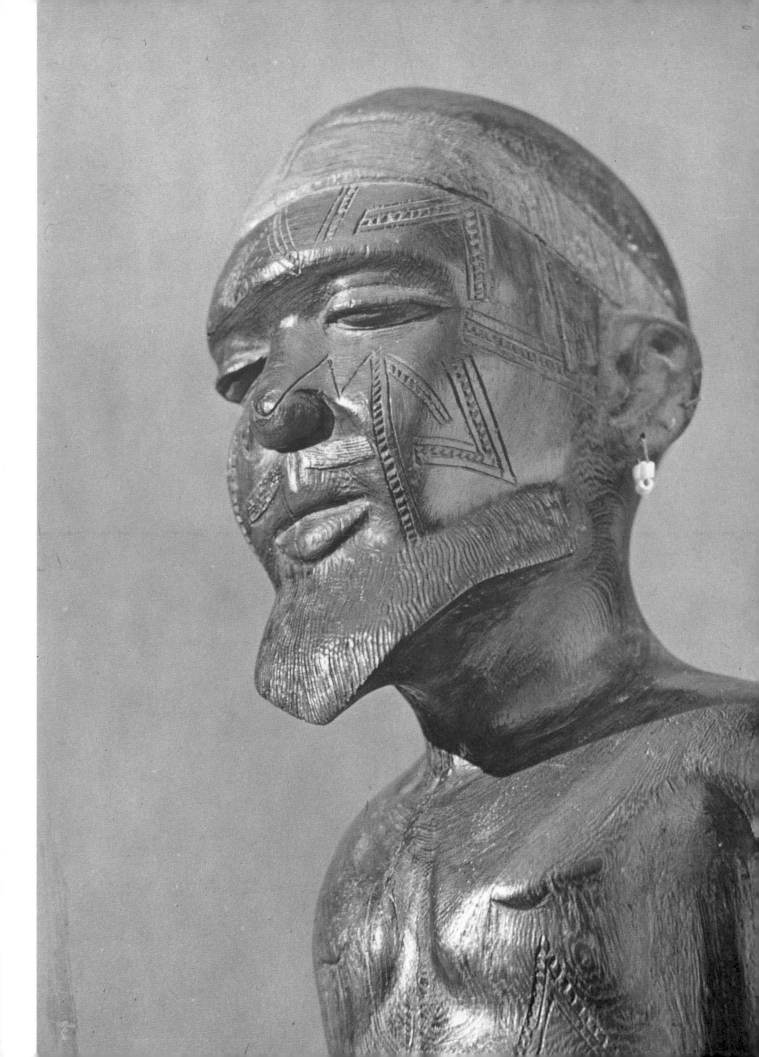

impersonated by a member of the society. The young men were taken one by one to a 'spirit', a masked robed figure, sitting on a tree trunk with the Poro horn, the pipe of office.

The Poro society is also found in neighbouring countries, and in Guinea this story is told of its origins. In the olden days there was a great famine and food was scarce and bad. There were some goods in the market but the women sellers demanded very high prices. The men got desperate, and at a secret meeting they decided to frighten the women away from the market and seize their provisions. So they carved human features on pieces of wood, put horns on some and horrid faces on others, and practised guttural sounds such as were never heard from human mouths. Then they went to the market, masked and screeching, while other masked figures interpreted their words. The frightened women gave them all they wanted and ran away. The masked figures beat all the men they met, and cut scars on their bodies, saying that this would assure their protection by the spirits. Since then men have made scars on their bodies and women always provide food for the masked Poro dancers.

These fanciful explanatory myths must not detract from the serious purpose of the Poro society. Its function is to fit every youth to play the role of an adult in society, and perpetuate the ancestral customs. The society is controlled by elders and arranged in a hierarchy, but differing in each village. It is said that the first Poro spirit before he died named

A figure of a woman and child from an altar of the Poro society, Sierra Leone. The Poro is one of the most celebrated African 'secret societies'. It serves to initiate youths into the tasks of manhood, and continues ancestral customs. Reproduced by kind permission of R. J. Hewett.

A head-rest from Mozambique, carved out of a single piece of wood like the better known stools; such head-rests were used in ancient Egypt. Antelopes and other deer appear in many African stories. A tale from Togo says that a chief wanted to show his superiority by riding an antelope and sent his hunters to catch one. But he did not know that it was really a ghost, and when he mounted it he was carried off at great speed into the forest and has never been seen since.

his wife as leader of the women's section. Since then women have joined on the same terms as men, but are not usually officials. The Poro members meet in 'sacred bush' outside the village, where the founder of the particular group was buried. The chief masked spirit is the Gbeni, who may only be looked at by members of the society, and appears in public on special occasions for example, when a new group of boys is to be initiated, in a series of rituals lasting from November till May.

The initiation is a symbolical rebirth. The youth is swallowed by the Poro spirit when leaving his parents; this is like death, and marks are cut on his back to indicate the scars left by the spirit's teeth. The boys stay in a camp, with no modern comforts, sleeping on the ground, staying out in the rain, cooking their own food, and making wild cries if they see village people. They are instructed in family and social duties, and learn drumming and Poro songs. At the end of the training they return to their parents as reborn, having passed from childhood to manhood.

A parallel society, the Sande, exists for the initiation of girls, with the same purpose of fitting them for adult life. The Sande spirit appears masked in public on great occasions, with a wooden mask, and a robe of black cloth covered with strips of wood fibre and little bells fixed on the dress. These masked figures, though terrifying at first sight, are known to represent the spirits of the ancestors and of the societies, and are deliberately meant to show their supernatural character and power over men.

A story about the origin of masks is told by the Kono people of Guinea. An old woman used to make pots and went one day to get supplies of clay from the banks of a little stream far from her village in the forest. Her daughter was with her and as the woman dug she placed the clay beside her daughter. Suddenly she dug up a Thing, which surprised her, but she put it by her daughter and went on digging. A little later she came upon another Thing, female this time, the first having been male. The two Things said not a word, though the woman tried to make them talk by pinching them. The daughter ran off to the village to fetch other women and when all had arrived they decided to take the Things home with them. When they got there they shut all the men up in their houses, with the exception of a doctor whom they wanted to help them persuade the Things to speak. He told them to put the Things in a hut and burn pepper there.

Before long the Things began to be stifled by the fumes of burning pepper, and the women heard a low growl from the male Thing, which said 'Shake your rattles!' At the sound of this voice the women fled, crying out to the men to save them. The men emerged from their houses and they heard the female Thing singing sweetly. They took charge of the Things, and have held the secrets of their voices and masks ever since, while the women who discovered them lost control of the masks through lack of courage.

Another version says that the women found the spirits under the large leaves of a climbing plant. They brought them home and danced round them, but were terrified when the Things began to growl in menacing tones. Their men came with weapons, took the spirits to the forest, and ever since have known the secrets of the masks though women discovered them first. The stories suggest an earlier dominance of women, which men later overcame.

Many of the societies use a bull-roarer. This is a flat piece of wood or metal, which when twirled at the end of a cord gives off an irregular and frightening sound. A story told by the Dogon of Upper Volta says that when the masked dancers performed the women came to watch, and

A mask of the small Baga tribe of Guinea. It represents the goddess of maternity, protector of mothers, worshipped by the Simo society. The head is carried on the dancer's head, and he sees through holes in the chest, while his body is completely covered by a fibre dress.

Page 100, left: this kettle drum stands on the head of a wooden cult figure. It is from the Bakongo, who live near the mouth of the Congo River, and whose natural style may be partly due to long contact with Europeans. However, the snakes on the drum and in the hand are of African inspiration. Horniman Museum.

Page 100, right: the Ekpe or Egbo is one of the principal societies of the Ibibio and neighbouring peoples of Eastern Nigeria. It is a club as well as a cult, but the main purpose is the worship of ancestors and the encouragement of fertility. The club-house has images and symbols of the spirits, like this figure.

Page 101: mask of the Poro society of Sierra Leone and Guinea. The members meet in 'sacred bush' to perform rituals for their ancestors and to initiate young men into adult secrets and duties. The masked spirits appear in public on great occasions when the whole body is covered with cloth or grass.

even when men tried to chase them away the women peered from far off and imitated the dances. Then a man called Moyna found a flat piece of iron at the smithy. He tied a cord to it, and whirled it in the air and was struck by the sound it made.

On the night of the next dance there was a low growling sound, and the women looked round in fear, wondering what it was. Moyna whirled it faster and the women fled in panic. Next day Moyna got the blacksmith to make a better piece of iron, with a hole at the end. At night-time he went outside the village and whirled his bull-roarer faster than before. The women fled into the safety of their houses and Moyna went through the village, announcing that it was the Great Mask speaking, and any women or children who came out would be eaten. Since that day women and children always hide indoors when the bullroarer sounds. When Moyna died he passed the secret to his sons, and told them to sound the bull-roarer when any notable person died.

The rock paintings that are found in many parts of Africa often depict animals and men, and sometimes masked figures. A Dogon story says that a leopard was pursuing its prey, a gazelle. The chase became furious as the gazelle fled for its life and soon the two were far from their home in the bush. They came into rocky country and lost their way. But the chase continued fast and fierce, until the beasts found themselves confronted with a high and long wall of rock that even they could not leap over. So great was their speed that they both crashed into the wall and flattened themselves on it. Their pictures can still be seen, the smaller representing the gazelle, and the leopard with his neck and legs elongated by his speed. Another story says that a woman had seen masked dancers

A dance mask in carved and painted wood from Dahomey. Such masks are worn during ceremonies performed to ward off the influence of sorcerers. Collection Bastide.

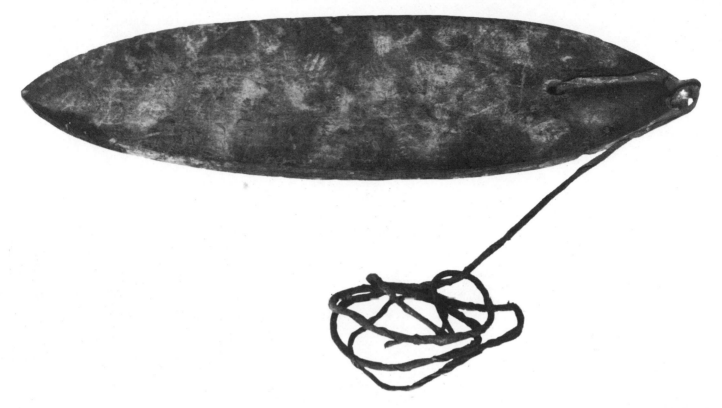

and wanted to get hold of the pattern of their masks, so she drew it on the ground and her husband copied it on the rocks. More often it is said that the painting was made by an ancestor or a hero who wanted to teach his descendants the form of masks that he had learnt from spiritual beings. And more simply, but perhaps no less truly, rock paintings are said to represent some outstanding event, or simply just some curious being.

Myths of the ancestors will be found under stories about the first men, and in the next section on legends from different parts of Africa. Stories of the gods have shown that they are often partially ancestors, and a further example may be given from the Songhay of the upper Niger. Zoa was a wise man and ancestor of the people and their protector. Once he heard some travellers say that if a pregnant woman is given sheep's liver to eat, it is the child in her belly who is eating it. He tried this on a slave, cut open her belly, and saw the child eating. Another day Zoa went hunting and came across a wounded lioness lying on an ant-hill. Zoa tended the wound and after that the lioness went hunting with him. When Zoa married and had a son he took the boy hunting with him. They saw a bird eating millet and Zoa said that the bird would fall dead at his word, and it did so. He said that the bird should be cooked on a fire, and a fire lit itself and cooked the bird.

But his son began to cry at the death of the bird and Zoa, in anger. told the earth to open. He called all the people of the village to the edge of the hole, and told them that his son would be chief in future. When the rains would not fall, or evil came, or war happened, they must bring a white sheep or a white bull and offer it to him, and he would do all they asked. But he forbade the deaf, the blind, bastards, and all people with hernias to visit his shrine. Then he disappeared into the earth and closed it up after him, and four trees grow in that place, in the directions of the compass. Every year people have gone to pay homage to Zoa, and when there is no harvest they have prayed and he has given them millet. If they have been spared from war it is because he had prevented it.

A bull-roarer from the Nandi tribe of Kenya. Many African secret societies use this kind of instrument, which is found in other parts of the world also. When whirled rapidly in the air it gives off a harsh and irregular sound, like a bull roaring or a dog barking, which is said to resemble the uncanny voices of spirits of the dead. British Museum.

Legends of Old Africa

A myth is a story of supernatural or primeval beings which cannot be placed in recorded history. A legend is a traditional story, about historical or semi-historical people, even if the narratives are partly imaginary, and many stories include both myth and legend. No doubt every African people has legends of the founders of the group, or later heroes. Most of these are of great interest as illustrating thought and religion, as well as history and prehistory. Some well known stories are given here, selected from different parts of the continent.

The Golden Stool

Stools are traditional seats and symbols. In some places a man's personal stool is regarded as the shrine of his soul, and in funeral ceremonies it is carried into the family stool house, where regular offerings are made to the spirit of the ancestor. Stools are often highly carved, out of one block of wood, and there are many patterns all of which have a name and meaning.

In the eighteenth century the fourth king of Ashanti, Osai Tutu, made his people into a great nation. They had been subject to a neighbouring kingdom, whose ruler had a clansman called Anotchi. Anotchi offended that king and fled the country. He took up the study of medicine and magic and became the greatest doctor in the land. He said that Nyame, the supreme God, had given him the mission to make Ashanti a great people. He went to King Osai Tutu, and by means of his spiritual powers brought down from the sky, in a black cloud and amid thunder and dust, a wooden stool covered with gold. It slowly descended, to rest on the king's knees, and the monarch had four bells made to hang on each side of the stool. Anotchi told the king and the people that this Golden Stool contained the soul of the Ashanti people and that their health and welfare were in it. He made the king, queens and chiefs take a few hairs from their bodies and nails from their forefingers. These were made into magical powder, some of which was drunk and some poured on the stool. Anotchi said that the stool must not be sat upon, though on great occasions the king might pretend to sit on it three times and rest his arm on it. When it went out in procession once a year it was carried under umbrellas and attended with royal state.

The Ashanti rebelled against their oppressors and totally routed them. It is said that the king of that country was sitting playing the game of *wari* (mankala, a popular African game) with one of his wives, wearing gold chains on his wrists, when the Ashanti soldiers burst in upon him. The royal couple were executed and the golden chains fastened to the Golden Stool. Another king had a copy of the Golden Stool made for himself, and the Ashanti were so angry that they made war on him, and had two golden masks made from his face and attached to the Golden Stool.

When the British fought Ashanti in 1896 it was feared that the Golden Stool would be damaged, so Ashanti submitted. But the new conquerors

Left: rock paintings are found in many parts of Africa and this lavish example from Mtoko Cave, Rhodesia, is attributed to the Bushmen who were once here. Large elephants and other animals are easily recognisable but human figures are stylised without clear faces, which suggests that the painters only aimed at helping the chase of animals by magical means. Animals play many roles in African story and this picture is crowded with them, suggesting the flourishing wild life which is chiefly seen in certain reserves and game parks today. Frobenius Institute.

demanded to sit on the Stool, thinking it to be the sign of government. A second war broke out in which many lives were lost and the Golden Stool disappeared. It was not heard of again until 1921. Then some workmen making a new road came upon two brass pans. Before they could dig them up the custodians of the Stool came and frightened the men away, knowing that the hiding place of the Stool had been discovered. They said the place was infected with smallpox, and the Stool was taken to a new hiding place. But greedy people discovered it and stole gold ornaments from the Stool and tried to sell them. They were recognized and there was a great uproar; the thieves were put in prison to save their lives. National mourning was declared and a revolution seemed imminent. Fortunately the authorities had learnt the significance of the Golden Stool, and it was restored to the royal palace at Kumasi, where it remains. When Princess Mary was married in 1922 the Queen Mothers of Ashanti sent her a silver stool, with a message saying that their love was 'bound to the stool with silver fetters, just as we are accustomed to bind our own spirits to the base of our stools'.

Ifé Art

The wealth of art found at Ifé in Nigeria has only become known to the wider world in the last few years. So much of the rest of African art seems stylized that the calm naturalism of the Ifé bronzes and terracottas makes a great contrast. The bronzes are usually dated from the thirteenth or fourteenth centuries and show the existence of schools of craftsmen whose works have rarely been rivalled before or since. Other work has

The state stool of King Kofi of Ghana, taken from his palace in Kumasi in 1873. Made of wood, covered with silver, it is the commonest pattern of royal stool. The centre is like a rainbow, and a proverb says that 'the circular rainbow encircles the neck of the nation'.

been done in ivory, clay and wood, and there are some fine royal stools in quartz.

The Yoruba regard Ilé Ifé, the 'house of Ifé' as their place of origin, as told in the creation myths (see page 20). Another version of this story says that when Great God had been sent to earth he became very thirsty and drank palm wine, and lay down to sleep. As he was away a long time God sent his brother Odu-duwa to continue the work of creation. This he did and supplanted Great God in ownership of the land. Oduduwa is regarded as the first king of Ifé and the founder of their race. He was a strong personality but little has survived about him except general stories.

The son of Oduduwa was Oranyan who was a great warrior. In old age he retired into a grove, but if his people were attacked he emerged and dispersed enemies single-handed. One day, however, during a festival when the city was full of people and some were drunk, a man called out to Oranyan that they were being attacked. The old king came out on horseback and laid about the crowd, until the people begged him to stop destroying his own subjects. Then the shocked warrior drove his staff into the ground and said he would never fight again. It is said that it was turned to stone and so were he and his wife. Broken remains of stone have been dug up and fitted to restore the pillar, 'the staff of Oranyan', which stands about twenty feet above ground, and studded with iron nails the pattern and meaning of which are disputed.

The later history of Ifé is not yet well documented, except for the fine bronze heads of kings which are still being unearthed. One of the best known is the Olokun head, discovered at Ifé in 1910, which represents a king, or the god of the sea whose clay images are still made in the region today.

Benin Bronzes

The craftsmanship of Ifé was passed on to the kingdom of Benin, which being nearer the sea was better known to early European travellers. Some of the early heads and royal masks are of modified naturalism. One of the best known is an ivory mask still worn by the king of Benin on ceremonial occasions. But from the sixteenth century Benin art developed in a baroque direction and became more elaborate and stylized.

Myths of Benin say that their kingdom was founded by the youngest son of the supreme God. His elder brothers founded Ifé and other realms. When they left heaven each son was permitted to take some valuable object with him that would be useful on earth. The others chose tools, wealth and magic. But a bird told the youngest son to take a snail shell. When the sons arrived on the watery marsh here below the bird told the youngest to turn up the snail shell, and sand fell out which covered the marsh. The debt of this story to the Yoruba creation myths is obvious. It justified the title of the king of Benin to the marshy land on which his realm was founded.

Myths say that the first people of Benin could not agree among themselves and for a time they were without rulers. At last they sent to the king of Ifé, Oduduwa, and asked him to send one of his sons to rule over them. Some say it was this son who brought the snail shell that gave him authority over the land, and the snail is modelled in brass and preserved in the royal palace. The son is said to have been Oranyan, whose stone staff is at Ifé. But after some years he renounced the rule of Benin

A famous bronze head from Ifé, Nigeria, where some of the finest African art flourished from the thirteenth century A.D. Sometimes called after Ol-okun, god of the sea, the head probably represents an early king.

The elaborate prow of a canoe from Douala, Cameroun. European figures and mythological motifs are combined in a design of remarkable vitality. Very striking is the encounter of the bird and the snake in the fore part. Museum für Völkerkunde, Munich.

in favour of his son and returned home. The date of the foundation of this kingdom is generally put in the twelfth or thirteenth century.

Brass-casting was brought to Benin from Ifé in the fourteenth century, and in 1472 the first Europeans arrived, one of the Portuguese expeditions on their voyages of discovery round Africa. The fifteenth king of Benin was then on the throne; the present monarch is the thirty-fifth of the dynasty.

In the sixteenth century, Benin art developed away from naturalism and became more elaborate, though still expressing meaning and not just stylized for its own sake as in some of the later art. Bronze panels were cast containing a number of figures. Some of them depict Olokun, the god of the sea and wealth (see page 83). Story connects him with a king who became paralysed in the legs and gave out that he had become the Sea God. Thereafter on bronze panels two mudfishes are shown in place of the king's legs. Other bronzes showed the pointed headdress and the high collar imitating the red coral bead crowns and necklets of the kings.

The Benin artists soon showed their adaptability by including figures who are clearly in Portuguese dress and carrying fire-arms. They show the impression made by Europeans and the skill of the artists in depicting new types. Bronze and wood work still continues, though much commercialized. Some of the most lively arts are those that cannot be exported, wooden posts carved for ancestral graves, and mud sculptures which are popular but fragile. There are mud reliefs on palaces and houses in Benin, comparable to those in old Dahomey though not so ancient. They give striking representations of kings and courtiers, soldiers and musicians, masked dancers and animals.

Spear Masters

Among the Dinka people of the upper Nile the Spear Masters are a hereditary priesthood, and their importance is shown by myths which unite political and religious ideas. One version says that long ago there were dances held by lions, and a man was dancing there when a lion demanded his bracelet. He refused, whereupon the lion bit off his thumb to get the bracelet and the man died. He left a wife who had a daughter but no son and she went weeping to a river. A river spirit asked why she was crying, and hearing that she had no son he told the woman to lift her skirt and brush the waves towards her so that they could enter her. He gave her a spear, the symbol of bearing a male child, and a fish for food, and told her to return home without delay. The woman bore a son called Aiwel, who had a full set of teeth at birth, a sign of spiritual power.

When he was still a baby his mother left him asleep on the floor, and on coming back she found that a full gourd of milk had been drunk. She accused her daughter of having stolen the milk and punished her. The same thing happened again and the mother became suspicious. She pretended to leave the baby alone with the milk and went out, but hid herself to watch him. She saw Aiwel get up from the floor and drink the milk. When she burst in and accused him, the child warned her not to tell anybody, else she would die. But the woman could not keep the secret to herself, and she died as Aiwel had predicted, for he already had the power of spear-masters in making his word come true, however terrible.

After his mother's death Aiwel would no longer live with his family

The Staff of Oranyan, second king of the Yoruba of Nigeria. It is said that the king thrust his staff into the ground, where it turned into this stone pillar twenty feet high which still stands at Ifé. It is studded with iron nails in a pattern whose meaning is unknown. The white band and the pot at the base show that offerings have been made.

and he went to stay with his spirit-father in the river until he grew up. Then he returned from the river as a man with an ox of many colours, representing great wealth and the colours of all the herds; but his chief colour was that of the rain clouds. The ox was called Longar, and from then on the man was called Aiwel Longar. He took up his abode in the village, tending the cattle that had belonged to his mother's first husband, who had died of the lion's bite. There came a drought on the land and people had to take their cattle far afield to find grass and water. Many of them became thin and died, but the cattle of Aiwel were fat and strong. The young men decided to spy on him to find out where he fed and watered them. They followed him to where some long-rooted grass was growing, and there he pulled up tufts of the grass to give his cattle the water that was underneath. Aiwel knew that the young men had spied on him and again his secrets were fatal, for when the youths revealed them to others they all died.

Aiwel Longar then told the village elders to leave their land where the cattle would die, and said he would take them to a promised land where there was inexhaustible pasture and water and no death. But the elders did not believe him and set off on their own. So Aiwel went by himself, but it seems the people tried to follow him after all, for God put barriers of great mountains and rivers in their way. At one river where they

A favourite African game, known by its Egyptian name of Mankala. This fine board from Sierra Leone shows the twelve holes in each of which four nuts are placed. The two players sit on opposite sides and distribute the nuts all round the board in turn. If a turn ends at holes that already contain one or two nuts the contents are taken by the player. He puts the nuts in one of the containers at each end, and the one who gains most nuts wins.

Right, above: a very old and venerated drum beaten by the kings of Buganda on their accession. The snake shown in relief commemorates the victory of the founder of the race over the king of snakes.

Right, below: wooden mask of the Bobo, Upper Volta, fringed with hair and raffia. The horns, facial marking, and white face suggest the power and strangeness of the spirit it represents. The body of the human wearer is entirely concealed by the robe.

tried to cross, Aiwel stood on the other side and killed the men with his fishing-spear as they passed over. The people were in danger of being destroyed altogether, until a man called Agothyathik made a ruse to save them. One of his friends took a large ox bone and held it out on a pole in front of him as he went through the reeds on the river bank. When Aiwel saw this he thought it was a human head and prepared to spear it. While he was occupied Agothyathik crept round to the back and grappled with him. For a long time they wrestled, till Aiwel was tired and gave up. He told Agothyathik to call the people over. Some were afraid, but to those who came Aiwel gave fishing-spears to carry when they prayed, and war spears. He gave them other divinities to worship, and a sky-coloured bull whose thigh-bone would be sacred to them.

The men who received these gifts from Aiwel founded the clans which are now spear-masters, 'people of the fishing-spear'. Others who came later were 'people of the war-spear' and founded warriors clans. Aiwel Longar then left the spear-masters to rule the country, and said he would not intervene except in time of trouble.

There are other versions of this myth. One says that in the beginning all the people lived in the river, and the first to emerge was called Longar, the eldest son of God. He was like a spirit and like a man, the first to be created and the source of all life. Despite differences in the versions there are common themes, particularly the conflict with the divine figure who tries to kill the founder of the clan at a river-crossing, but who is outwitted and in the end gives his blessing. The fishing-spear is the symbol of the priesthood, as explained by the myth. It shows that the original spear-master was a river man. Death and its avoidance also figure in the stories, as well as the land and its ownership, which continues to be of the first importance for life.

Facing Mount Kenya

The Kikuyu, or more correctly, *Gikuyu*, people of Kenya say that in the beginning the Divider of the Universe, the creator God, made a great mountain as a sign of his wonders and a resting place for himself. This was Kere Nyaga, the 'mountain of Brightness' or mystery, which Europeans call Mount Kenya. This was the earthly dwelling place of God, whose person cannot be seen and who is far away, though he is invoked at the crises of life. Men turn towards the mountain in prayers, lift up their hands and offer sacrifices there.

One myth says that God gave a choice to his three sons who were the fathers of the Kikuyu, Masai and Kamba peoples. He offered them a spear, a bow and a digging-stick. Masai chose the spear and was told to tend herds on the plains, Kamba chose the bow and was sent to the forest to hunt game, while Gikuyu selected the digging-stick and was taught the ways of agriculture. Another version says that God took Gikuyu to the top of the mountain and showed him the land with its valleys, rivers, forests, game, and all that God had made. Right in the middle of the country was a place where fig trees clustered and God told Gikuyu to make his home there.

When he got to the spot Gikuyu found that not only had God made a fine place, but he had also provided a wife for him. She was a beautiful woman, called Moombi, the Moulder or Creator and she bore nine daughters to her husband.

Gikuyu was happy at this, but he could not help grieving that he had no sons. So he went to the mountain and called on God, asking his help. God told him not to worry but to follow his instructions. Gikuyu was to take a lamb and a kid, and sacrifice them under a large fig tree near his house. The fat and blood of the animals were to be poured on the trunk of the tree, and the meat to be given to God by all the family as a burnt offering. Gikuyu did as God had directed and then took his wife and daughters home. When they got to the fig trees they found to their joy nine young men there. Gikuyu killed a ram and prepared millet for a great feast. They all ate, rejoiced, and then slept for the night. In the morning Gikuyu put the question of marriage to the young men. He offered them his daughters, but made the condition that if they accepted they must all live in his home, under the system of matriarchal or female descent. The youths agreed willingly.

Then the Kikuyu all lived together in one group, which was named after the mother of them all, the family group of Moombi. When the parents died, the property was shared out equally among the daughters. Finally numbers became too great and the nine daughters each called her family together and made a clan bearing her own name. So were founded the

A sixteenth-century Benin bronze figure of an archer. The cross is Portuguese and could have been acquired to be worn simply as a decoration, while the coral beads and skirt edged with a chain motif are characteristic of this part of Africa.

chief Kikuyu clans, each still known by the names of the nine daughters, and the whole being of the tribe of Moombi.

The women of Moombi's tribe practised polyandry, having several husbands each, a practice found in some other places, though it is more common for men to have several wives, a system called polygyny or generally polygamy. It seems that the men suffered under the women, they were afflicted with sexual jealousy and often guilty of infidelity, and they were punished and humiliated. So they planned to revolt, though it was not easy, since the women were strong and good fighters. The men made a secret plot, which brought nature on their side, and was both ingenious and pleasurable. They all made love to the women and awaited results. After six months it was clear that nature had helped their plan and the women were in the family way. The men then broke out in open revolt and the women were too burdened to resist. So the men became heads of the community. They abolished polyandry, and instituted polygyny, taking several wives each. They also decided to change the names of the tribe and clan. The group of Moombi became the Nation of Gikuyu, their first father. But when the men tried to alter the names of the female clans, the women in turn revolted. They threatened to kill all the male children that might be born to them, and to refuse to bear any more children after that. So the men had to yield, and the Kikuyu clans are still known by the names of the women who were the first founders of the clan system.

Time passed, families multiplied, and there was not enough room for everybody in the original Kikuyu settlement. Some of the people moved into the forest to get more land, but entry was barred for a time by Pygmies who lived there in caves under the ground. They were shy, and dug tunnels under the earth to avoid meeting people. The Kikuyu thought they were magicians who could open up the ground and disappear at will. In time they disappeared, though stories are still told of little people underground. They were probably driven out by a race of hunters, Ndorobo, who traded animal skins and flesh and honey to the Kikuyu, in exchange for grain and fruit. When the Kikuyu wanted more land they bought it from the Ndorobo, so they not only had the plains which God had given them but forest land which they had bought.

The Inventor King

The Bushongo and related tribes of the Congo tell of the beginnings of their people with an old man and his wife who had no children. One day the sky opened and a man of white colour came towards them. He asked where the other people were, and they replied that there were none and they were too old to have children. The visitor said he was the Lord, called Bomazi, and that a child would be born to them. The old folks laughed, but soon the woman gave birth to a girl, and when she was grown up the light-skinned Bomazi took her for wife. They had five sons, all of whom became chiefs of different peoples.

The first two children were twins, Woto and Moelo. When they grew up Woto had three wives, but coming back from the hunt one day he found his brother's son with his own wife and accused him of incest. The boy begged forgiveness but Woto found him sinning in turn with his other two wives. Woto was angry and went away into the forest, bewailing his loneliness. He was a magician and at his songs the forest trees opened and many little people came out of them. They exclaimed at the size of Woto; what big ears he had, what big eyes and nose. Nobody could subdue such a man, only women could enslave him. These were of course the Pygmies.

Woto wandered on and in time became father of all the Bushongo. But the stories are vague about his successors until the accession of the great king Shamba Bolongongo, said to be the ninety-third ruler, who lived about 1600 A.D. He is called Shamba of the Bonnet, and many inventions are credited to him. While still heir to the throne Shamba told his mother that he wanted to travel abroad to see other peoples. She warned him of the dangers, but Shamba replied that the king must be the wisest of men, and only by travelling could he learn about other people, admire what was good and learn to prevent what was evil. So he visited many countries, and came back after several years to introduce useful things that he had seen.

Shamba showed his people how to weave raffia fibre for clothing, in place of the rough bark cloth they had been using. He introduced the cassava plant, which the Portuguese had brought from America, and which needs long preparation to get rid of its poisons. He showed them embroidery and other crafts. Till then the Bushongo had been addicted to gambling, but Shamba showed them how to play the game of Mankala, which came originally from the Arabs.

Shamba was a man of peace. He abolished bows and arrows for warfare, and particularly the terrible weapon called the *shongo*. This was a throwing knife with four blades, which caused horrible wounds. Because of his peaceful ways Shamba and his people were respected and they were able to travel widely. If strange people attacked them, they had only to say that they were Bushongo and the thieves knelt to them as subjects of Shamba. But if it happened that a Bushongo was killed by brigands, then Shamba sounded the war-horn and his people swarmed out like locusts to find the criminals. Even then enemies were not killed unless they resisted, and women and children were spared. Shamba said that all men were children of God and had the right to live.

The Bushongo attribute almost all good things to Shamba. He introduced tobacco, and the oil palm tree bears the name Shamba. It is said that he compared palm wine to human nature, one of his many parables with a moral. When the first cut is made in a palm tree the wine is sweet but very weak, but as the flow increases it becomes stronger but harsh. That is like human life, youth is sweet but lacks wisdom, while old age is wise but lacks sweetness.

Many stories are told of Shamba's wisdom, and his judgements are remembered. If a guilty party did not appear in court he lost his case, because Shamba had said that a guilty man tries to avoid discussing matters. If a witness related hearsay and had not seen things himself, he was rebuked because Shamba had said that only he should speak who had seen with his own eyes. To bring peace to quarrelling wives Shamba told a story of a man who had two dogs, one black and the other red. Every day after his own meal he divided the rest into equal shares and gave them to the dogs. One day when a wild cow had been killed by the villagers the man was given a thigh bone for his share. He enjoyed the meat and gnawed away till only the bone was left. He tried to break it to get at the marrow, but it was too hard and he threw it to the dogs. Both dogs tried to grab the bone, and turned on each other in fury, fighting so hard that they died of wounds. Shamba said that each dog should have his own bone, and each woman her own husband, and then there would be peace at home.

One of the beautiful ivory carvings which resulted from the meeting of African and European cultures in the sixteenth century. The African feeling is powerful and snakes and crocodiles can be seen. But the ivory also carries the arms of the Portuguese royal house, religious motifs, and a palpably European hunting scene.

A famous Bushongo wood carving shows King Shamba seated in front of a Mankala board, his body decorated to show armlets and clothing, the hands roughly done, but all the attention is drawn to the face in its wisdom and peace.

Kintu and his Successors

The myth of Kintu has been told as the first man of Buganda, with a heavenly wife (pages 41-3). When he was an old man Kintu went into the forest and disappeared. It was taboo for the chiefs to say that he had died, so they said he had vanished. They dug his grave secretly behind his house. The body was wrapped in cow-hide and put in the grave without

Mount Kenya, 17,000 feet high, the Mountain of Brightness, which the Kikuyu say God chose as his earthly dwelling place. From here God showed the first man all the land that he had made, and told him to make his home in a cluster of fig trees in the centre.

any earth on top, but thorns were placed over and around it as protection against wild beasts. The chief priest kept watch on the grave until he was able to remove Kintu's jawbone (a sacred bone, because it moves by itself), and this was put in a hill temple. The temple and its garden are sacred and animals may not be killed there; the ghosts of Kintu and his son act as guardians against wrong.

Kintu's son who succeeded him was also said to have been lost, this time on the plains. He was followed as king by his grandson Kimera. Kimera's mother was the wife of a neighbouring king, but who committed adultery with a visiting prince. Her lover died and she was saved from the King's anger by the help of a priest. This man said he had received a divine message to tell the king that if he heard of the misconduct of one of his wives he must not kill her, but banish her from the palace, and when her child was born throw it into a pit. This was done, but the child was saved from the clay pit by a potter, who could not bring up the child himself, but entrusted it to a nobleman whose wife cared for it. The child was Kimera, and when Buganda needed a new king they called for him and he was crowned. His mother came with him, but she stayed in a house outside the capital.

After some years Kimera sent an expedition, headed by his son, against a rich neighbour. The son died on the way, leaving a child called Tembo. When Tembo grew up his mother told him that his father had been killed by his grandfather, Kimera. She so worked on Tembo's feelings that he began to watch for an opportunity of killing his grandfather. One day the king was out hunting and got separated from his bodyguard. Tembo seized his chance, crept up behind the king and killed him with a club. He told the people that it was an accident, and that he had hit the king while aiming at an animal. The king's jawbone was enshrined on another hill, and Tembo succeeded him.

Some time later Tembo sent his son and daughter to be servants of one of the gods. But the young man became enamoured of his sister, they were united and she gave birth to twins. At the places where the children were conceived and born rivers sprang forth (see page 87). Later on Tembo became insane, but was cured by a human sacrifice, and he wore anklets from the sinews of a man from the fish clan. His jawbone was preserved in another temple.

Some thirty kings of Buganda followed, and only a few can be mentioned for their legends. The sixteenth king, Juko, so angered a priest that the latter commanded the sun to fall. Darkness covered the land, till one of the king's wives suggested that he should send for a god who lived on an island in Lake Victoria. The god came (or his priest and symbols), and restored the sun to its place. Then the king's brother took a wife against the advice of the priests, with the result that a child was born without arms or legs, which was said to be an incarnation of the god of plague. To appease the god a temple was built for him, but the king was told never to look at it. For some years he obeyed, but later he forgot, and died after looking at the forbidden shrine.

The children of the eighteenth king died in infancy, and he was in despair. Then he was told by priests to restore a neglected temple, and after that his children survived. But the priests demanded enormous sums for their services, and the king was so angry that he ordered all the temples of the gods to be plundered and burnt down. Then he fled to the forest, but his people brought him back. It was found that he was possessed by the spirit of the greatest of the gods, Mukasa, and could give oracles. So the people built him a new palace where he lived and died.

Zimbabwe. Two of the massive conical towers flanking a gateway.

It is said that the twenty-second king of Buganda was summoned with his queen by the ghost of the first king, Kintu. But just as they got to his temple another chief came up and Kintu's ghost fled. Later in his reign the king received a lying message that one of the old kings had risen from the dead and was coming to fight him. He sounded the war drums, and there was great confusion and slaughter among his people. A further revolt was encouraged by a priest who said that whoever stood on a magical charm would reach the throne, so the princes rebelled and killed the king.

The greatest monarch was Mutesa, the thirtieth, both competent and ambitious. He built up a large army, with troops from every district, and introduced guns. His merchants brought back cottons, in exchange for ivory and slaves. Both Moslems and Christians entered the country during his reign, but modern times came and the slave trade was eventually destroyed.

The Zimbabwe Mystery

The mythology of the great Zimbabwe stone buildings is at present more European than African, yet they are important both for that and for their place in the expression of African art. Seventeen miles south-east of Fort Victoria in Rhodesia are three main groups of stone buildings that were made famous in Rider Haggard's *King Solomon's Mines*. Stone constructions are so unusual in ancient tropical or southern Africa that writers have suggested they were built by Arabs, Jews, Indians, Chinese, in fact anybody but Africans. Similarly the naturalistic bronzes of Ifé used to be a attributed to some castaway Portuguese, and it was not known then that comparable sculptures were made at Nok in Nigeria two thousand years ago. In fact over three hundred stone ruins have been found in Rhodesia and neighbouring countries. All scholars are now agreed that the Zimbabwe ruins were the work of African builders, from the ninth century to the fifteenth. They were known to Portuguese travellers from 1513. That Indian and Chinese fragments have been found in the excavations simply shows that trade was going on through the Arabs whose boats plied between the coasts of Africa and Asia.

Zimbabwe lies in the country now occupied by the Shona people and they seem to have few stories linking them with the ruins. One of the Portuguese writers said that the people in his day ascribed these buildings to the Devil, but African mythology has no Devil in the Christian sense. Later travellers were told that long ago white men put up the buildings but black men poisoned the water and they all died. These seem likely to have been tales invented to please Europeans, and Africans are often reluctant to reveal their own traditional history. It may well be that the Zimbabwe buildings were made by other African tribes, or groups of tribes, who later moved further south, such as the Venda of Transvaal.

An empire led by Monomotapa in the sixteenth century included a number of tribes. According to Shona myths, fire was unknown to their ancestors until brought by the Rozwi, rulers of a large kingdom, perhaps the same domain as that of Monomotapa. They also brought grains and other seed. They lived in Zimbas, or Zimbabwe, a name which was applied to the residences or burial places of leading chiefs. There were many of these Zimbabwes, which were occupied by Rozwi until recent times. But in the tribal and European wars of the nineteenth century the old kingdoms were broken up and many peoples left their ancient homes. Shaka the Zulu was extending his rule in South Africa, and the Matabele, though a powerful people, fled north and in turn went through the land of the Shona and the Zimbabwes. The end of this culture was due to wars and European occupation.

The nature of the ruins at Great Zimbabwe has been confused by romantic interpretations. There are three main groups: the largest is an elliptical 'temple' enclosing a conical tower, a fortified 'acropolis', and a mass of smaller stone enclosures called 'valley ruins'. There are stone carvings and a number of soapstone birds which are unusual, but wooden bird effigies on poles are to be found among a number of Bantu peoples today, the lightning being thought of as a giant bird.

In the ruins of the stone forts of Zimbabwe are numerous stone carvings, including a number of soapstone birds, similar to wooden figures found today among some Bantu people of South Africa. Lightning is thought to be like a giant bird.

There are soapstone bowls, decorated, with patterns of animals and geometrical designs, which resemble the wooden bowls used for divination by the Venda (see page 89). Perhaps some day a fuller African mythology will be recorded of Zimbabwe, or it may be lost for ever, leaving only the artistic works as evidence of the thought of vanished African peoples.

Rain-Queen

The Lovedu are a Bantu tribe of the Transvaal, not numerous, but notable for their Rain-Queen, Mujaji. The character of this queen, and the nature of the country where she ruled, suggested a theme and provided a location for Rider Haggard which he realised in the famous romance called *She*. Haggard suggested she must be of Arab stock but he knew little of the history.

The Lovedu have few cosmological myths. A rare story speaks of Khuzwane, who created the world and man, and left his footprints on rocks in the north while they were still soft. Another deity, sometimes identified with the first, is blamed for troubles such as sterility, and is a kind of destiny. But the chief object of rituals is the well-being of the family and the honouring of tribal ancestors.

About A.D. 1600, somewhere in the far north, the sons of a great king quarrelled and set up independent realms. One of them, Mambo, ruled in the area which is now called Rhodesia. Mambo's daughter bore a son, though she was unmarried. She refused to disclose her lover's name, saying that the father of a prince should not be known. Tradition says he was her brother. When Mambo threatened his daughter she stole the rain charm and the sacred beads and fled south with her son, where they founded the Lovedu tribe. The son's child was named Muhale and he became a great king. He invited relatives from the north to join him and help in clearing the forests, and in teaching the original inhabitants the use of fire. Many of these inhabitants actually perished in a great conflagration, possibly because they did not know how to control the new element. But the Lovedu were safe; they had in the meantime discovered the 'place of the gods', and had prayed there to appease the ancestors of the place.

The next king but one ruled in the mountains from a throne cut in the rock and surrounded by great walls, like those of Zimbabwe. He had a son, Mugodo, whom he treated like an outcast in public to deceive the people, but at night and in secret he taught him the secrets of the rain charms. However this disrespect brought division when Mugodo succeeded to the throne and his reign ended in confusion, terminating the rule of kings and inaugurating that of queens. Mugodo went to his favourite daughter and told her of a plan to save the kingdom, but she refused to believe that a sin could turn to good. Then he went to another daughter, Mujaji, and said that though unmarried she could give birth to the heir to the throne. She understood that Mugodo was to be the father and accepted his will. A daughter was born who became Mujaji II. For Mujaji I had already gained the ascendancy during her father's reign, but she lived in seclusion and hence men believed in her wisdom and immortality. She was called 'white-faced', 'radiant as the sun', 'one who gives water to wash the face'. Emissaries of other powers, the Sotho to the north and the Zulu to the south, came bringing gifts to the queen of the Rain-makers.

Mujaji II was not so successful and her land was invaded by Zulus

Mask of a white monkey called Ireli from the Dogon of Mali. The man who wears it leans on a stick and sits apart from the crowd in a melancholy attitude, but he is encouraged to dance by singers who chant: 'Monkey on a high tree full of fruit, all eyes are on you, the drum is beating for you, move your head, move your legs, all the people have their eyes on you.'

and Europeans. She tried to smite the Zulus with drought, and to deceive the Europeans by hiding herself and presenting a distant sister as 'She-who-must-be-obeyed'. But the sacred places were desecrated and in despair Mujaji II took poison and died. When Mujaji III came to the throne the Europeans discovered the previous deception and refused to recognize her till the other *She* had died. But conflict remained between the authority of the new conquerors and that of the Lovedu ancestors. However the Lovedu were one of the most peaceful in submission to the rule of the white people.

The Lovedu queen, now Mujaji IV, is more a rain-maker than a monarch, who gives rain to her own people and denies it to her enemies. She is 'transformer of clouds', who guarantees the cycle of the seasons, not only bringing rain in drought, but giving general care throughout the year. Her emotions, anger or satisfaction, are believed to affect her powers and help or hinder their working. People do not call on the queen every time rain fails, but in time of drought her advisers say that 'the people are crying'. They bring gifts and there are long dances. The queen does not work alone, but has a rain-doctor who tries to find the cause of drought by divination, and by his medicines tries to remove the forces which prevent the queen's powers from working. What objects and medicines she possesses are kept secret, for they are inherited and passed on to her successor just before the queen's death. There are also medicines which are burnt and produce black smoke to induce clouds to rise in the sky, as Elijah caused fire and smoke to appear on Mount Carmel and shortly afterwards rain came.

The Rain-queen herself can only control rain by agreement with her ancestors, whose skins are said to be the most important ingredients of her rain-pots. If rains do not fall it is said to be because the ancestors are angry at neglect. People still believe in the power of the queen to bring rain and her health is vital to the maintenance of good seasons. God gives the queen her powers, which have been shown in the appearance of needed storms.

An elaborate wooden mask of the Sande female initiation society of the Mende of Sierra Leone. Called Bundu, it represents the ancestors which preside over the girl initiates.

Swazi Kings

The Swazi people live to the north-east of South Africa. Names of their rulers go back thirty generations, though only the last eight can be clearly dated. There are many stories of early kings. One had two sons, Madlisa and Madlebe. The latter was son of a junior queen and was an unusual child; he was said to have been born wearing a magical bracelet, and when he wept tears of blood came and the bracelet cried in sympathy, 'Tsi, tsi!' One day the king called all his people and said that the son who could spit farthest he would make Little Chief. He hit them in turn with a hippo whip to make them spit far, but Madlisa's spittle only dribbled down his chest. Then the king hit Madlebe with his whip and his spittle went far away. There was a roar from the sky, Madlebe cried tears of blood, and the bracelet echoed 'Tsi, tsi!'

The king gave Madlebe a pot, a gourd and a spoon, and told him to place the pot on a high shelf for it must never be broken. One day Madlisa was hungry and tempted Madlebe to reach for the pot. At first he refused, but when he agreed and reached up the pot fell to the ground. The king was angry and sent his soldiers to execute Madlebe, who had fled to the forest. But when they lifted their hands to strike him the thunder roared and a lightning flash hit the earth. The warriors were afraid, and

As Others See Us

For nearly five hundred years Europeans have been trading with Africa, exploring it, and finally ruling over much of it for a time. These fair-skinned people with their strange ways have entered into African story. An amusing tale from Dahomey says that when the Europeans arrived they were always the first at the market, and would sit there all day long till everybody else had gone home. The local people wondered why this was and planned to find out. They got up in the night and went to the marketplace, and where the Europeans had been sitting were little holes. They filled these with black warrior ants and hid behind trees to watch. At dawn the Europeans arrived, sat down, then jumped up and ran off with wild cries. The Africans laughed to see that the traders had tails.

More seriously, in Kenya, it is said that a great doctor used to predict future events. One night he had a dream from which he awoke trembling and bruised all over. His family called the elders to find out the trouble. They made a sacrifice and gradually the doctor recovered his voice and told his dream. God had taken him to a distant land where he had seen strangers coming out of great waters, in colour like yellow frogs and with wings like butterflies. They carried sticks sending out fire by magic. They brought a great iron snake, like a centipede, which spat fire, and stretched from the sea to the great lake. The doctor warned his people not to fight the strangers, for that would bring disaster.

The elders and warriors were angry and said they would destroy the iron snake, but the doctor said they would not be able to do this, for it would repel their spears and arrows and destroy them in turn. The best thing to do would be to meet the strangers with courtesy but not to trust them, and especially not to bring them close to their homes and lands. But when Europeans did arrive, yellow and dressed in clothes like butterflies' wings, the Kikuyu did not know what to make of them. In time they forgot the advice of their prophet not to let the strangers come near their property. But they noticed that the yellow strangers were restless, they passed through the country, came and went, and never seemed to stay long in one place. So the Kikuyu recited a proverb which said that no mortal thing lived for ever, and no doubt the foreigners would return to their own land.

King Mugodo of the Lovedu (see page 118), before his reign ended in confusion, had the war horns sounded and danced a great solitary dance before his prostrate people. He prophesied the coming of black ants who would bite the people but would be overcome, and red ants who would fight and conquer the Lovedu. The black ants were the neighbouring warlike tribes and the red ants the Europeans. These came in the reign of his successors, the Lovedu queens. The black ants, the Zulus, were put off by the power of the queen in sending drought, and deception was tried on the red ants by presenting them with the wrong queen. This impostor was called 'Chief of the Reds' by the Lovedu themselves, and the Europeans refused to recognize the rightful queen until the impostor died. The Lovedu helped her to her end.

King Sobhuza of the Swazi is also said to have had a dream which foretold the coming of the invaders from Europe. They were strange people, the colour of red porridge, with hair like the tails of cattle. They had houses built on platforms and pulled by oxen. They spoke barbarous languages and were ignorant of human courtesies. They carried terrible weapons of destruction. The king's dream was interpreted

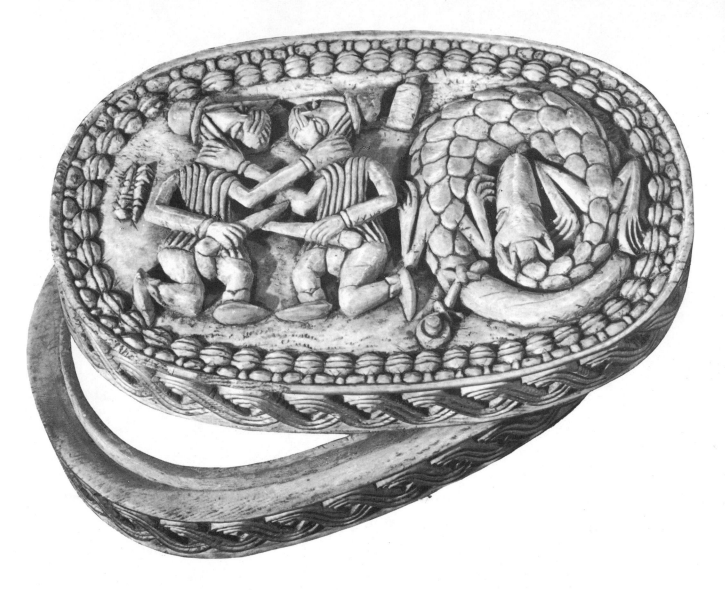

as a warning sent by his ancestors that he must never fight these foreigners, because of their great strength in battle. So it was that the Swazi
looked upon Europeans as useful allies, and that eventually they re-
quested the protection of England against other powers that threatened
them.

The prudence of the African rulers appears in all these stories. Europeans were strange people, of abnormal colour, hair, dress, manners and
needs. They were particularly to be treated with caution because of
their superior weapons. There was a good deal of politic evasion, which
was made easier by the ignorance of the Europeans of the customs of
the country.

Europeans tried to deal with the person they thought was king or
queen. But it was remarked in Ghana that they took no notice of the
old queen mother who crouched behind the king's throne and whispered
to him not to have any dealings with the strangers. Even those who
fought them, like Shaka, were willing to learn from European ways.
Kindness and hospitality, too, are as much a part of the ordinary African
people as the mythology suggests, and travellers like Livingstone jour-
neyed practically unarmed across the whole continent. There is also the
story of Mungo Park, who discovered the Upper Niger. When he was
alone and starving in the western Sudan, it was a simple old woman
who had pity on the stranger, took him in, and fed him like a child.

Europeans went to Africa from the end
of the fifteenth century onwards and did
not always agree among themselves.
This ivory box from Benin, Nigeria,
shows two Portuguese fighting, possibly
over possession of the crocodile seen on
the ground beside them.

Left: graceful antelope-like headdress, with seeds inlaid against the blue paint, made by the Kurumba of Upper Volta. It is used in a ceremony of dispersing ancestral spirits after a time of mourning.

Right: the Senufo of the Ivory Coast make many masks, half-human and half-animal. This figure of a standing bird has abstract patterns on the stylised wings, and genealogical figures on the back which suggest it was originally an ancestor-cult figure. Museum für Völkerkunde, Munich.

absent, and she prepared her excuses. When the Stag came to demand her reason the Goat said she had a kid. And the Stag then demanded if it was male or female. The Goat knew that the Stag's mother had died recently, so she said it was female. Then the Stag asked whose mother had been born again in the kid and the Goat replied that it was his own. The Stag could not harm the mother of his own reincarnated parent, so he went away.

Then the Antelope came along and asked why the Goat had been absent and was told that she had a male kid. When he demanded whose father had been reborn, he was told that it was his own, so he too went away. All the animals came in turn, and the Goat told each one that it was some dead relative of theirs reborn. But the Leopard was suspicious, and he hid while the Goat answered two other animals. To one he said he had a male kid and to the other a female. So when he came to the Goat's house and asked whose parent had been reborn, the Goat said it was his mother, because she knew the mother had died not long before. But the Leopard said it could be his father, who was also dead, and he respected him more. When the Goat tried to change her story, the Leopard sprang at her with a roar. The Goat leapt sideways out of her house and ran with all speed to the village of men. Only there did the Leopard turn back, and the Goat has stayed with men ever since, but the Leopard kills goats if it finds them straying outside a village.

Why the Tortoise is Taboo

A Malagasy fable says that one day a green Bird was hopping about in the bushes, looking for insects, when it saw a huge sea tortoise with a scaly shell come out of the water. The Tortoise told the Bird that it had always lived in the sea but would like to know the earth and its people. The Bird said that it was easily done and he would act as guide. So they set off for the interior. The Tortoise found it hard to walk, because of its flat feet, and began to complain. But the Bird had no trouble, jumping from tree to tree and resting in the shade. It laughed at the Tortoise at first, but then took pity on it. The Bird said it was a magician and would make better feet for the Tortoise. This was done and they went on with their journey. A little later the Bird dropped some dirt on the Tortoise, by accident, and the Tortoise called it filthy. The Bird got angry and flew off leaving the Tortoise to find its way back by itself. That is how the Sea Tortoise became a Land Tortoise. Ever since then the Land Tortoise and its children have wandered about, without finding the sea. So its flesh is taboo, for God made it for salt water, and men can only eat animals that live on land.

Tales of Spider and Hare

All across Africa fables are told of the cleverness, deceit and triumph of the Spider or the Hare, called by various names according to the language. These yarns were taken to America by the slaves and became the Brer Rabbit tales related by Uncle Remus. There are no rabbits in tropical Africa, and the clever animal is really a hare, which depends on its speed and cunning to protect itself against the dangers of the open Sudan and savannah country. Its chief enemy is the hyena, the Brer Fox of the American versions.

Right: mask of the Yoruba of Dahomey used in ancestor-cult societies and surmounted by a circular snake being attacked by a bird.

In the forest regions it is the Spider, the Annancy of America, which plays the role of the clever animal. In these stories the weak but guileful creature overcomes the powerful but stupid larger beasts. Perhaps he is the ordinary man, oppressed by harsh rulers or foreign conquerors, who projects himself into the parts of the agile hare or spider, taking revenge on the great ones of the earth. To score off the police or the government is a great delight, and always arouses laughter from the listeners to these village tales as they sit around in the moonlight. But they have their sad side too, and the hare who is caught in deception, or going beyond his powers, is severely punished by authority. Since he is often a thief or a practical joker, laughing at the morality of sober people, he suffers for his folly when caught.

Rubber Girl

This is a well known Hare or Spider tale, the Tar-baby of the Brer Rabbit stories. The Hausa of Nigeria tell it about the spider. One day the Spider told his wife to measure out some ground-nuts and he would plant them in his field. When they were ready he took his hoe, but arriving at the field he sat down by a shady stream, for it was hot and he was a lazy animal who preferred somebody else to work. He had a drink, began nibbling the nuts, finally ate them all, and fell asleep. When he awoke it was evening. He got some mud from the stream, plastered it all over his body, went home, and told his wife that he had come in dirty from work and wanted some water for a bath. The same thing happened on the following days, till the time for gathering the ground-nuts was at hand. Then the Spider's wife said that the neighbours were digging up their nuts and she would go and get their own. But her husband answered that as he had planted the nuts it was his right to dig them up. He went off and stole nuts from his neighbour's field, and did this so much that the neighbour kept watch and saw him.

Then he laid a trap for the Spider, in the form of a Rubber Girl made out of the sticky resin from the rubber tree. When the Spider came along he saw the Rubber Girl, with a beautiful long neck and large breasts. He came up to her, put out a hand and touched her breast, and his hand was held fast by the sticky rubber. 'Oh, you must want me badly,' he said, and put his other hand on her other breast. That hand stuck tight, and he exclaimed, 'You girls hold a man too tight. I will kick you.' He did this and the rubber caught his foot. Then he was angry and called the Rubber Girl an illegitimate child of low parents, and kicked her with the other foot. That stuck too and he was clasped tight to her body. He tried butting with his head and that stuck also to the Rubber Girl. Then the neighbour, who was watching from a hiding place, saw the Spider securely held and gave thanks to God. He cut a pliable switch from a tree, warmed it in a fire, rubbed it with grease, and beat and beat the Spider till his back was raw. Then he released the Spider and told him that if he came stealing again he would kill him. So the Spider suffered for his laziness and thieving.

In a Sierra Leone version the Spider wanted to eat rice but also to save himself the toil of working, so he pretended to die, having first made his wife promise to bury him on his farm. Then the rice from his neighbours' field started disappearing, for the Spider came out of his grave at night after the others had gone home, and ate all he found. His wife asked the advice of a diviner, who told her to make a girl of

The goat features in many African stories and often appears in art, as in this wooden carving from Cameroun.

wax from a tree that had sticky gum. The Spider was caught as before. Then all the people came up and beat him till the Spider's body became flat as it is today; formerly it was round and sleek.

In a Yoruba version of Nigeria the Hare figures in a tale of a great drought. All the animals decided that they would cut off the tips of their ears, and the fat from them would be used to buy hoes so that they could dig a well. Everyone did this except the Hare, who hid away. The other animals dug their well, and when it was finished the Hare came along beating a calabash, and making such a noise that the animals ran away without waiting to see who it was. Then the Hare drank his fill of water from the well, and not content with that he washed himself in the water and made it dirty. When he had gone the animals saw that they had been tricked, and they made an image of a girl and covered it with bird lime. The Hare was caught in the usual way and well beaten. Then he was driven away and has lived in the grasslands ever since, and that is why he has longer ears than any other animals.

In a version from Angola the owner of the farm was a Leopard, who made a wooden image of a girl and smeared it with gum from a wild fig-tree. He caught both the Hare and the Monkey, and gave them a thorough beating. Since then they have always slept in secret places to keep away from the Leopard; the Hare sleeping in a hole and the Monkey in a tree.

In southern African stories the Hare is caught by the Tortoise, who hid in the bottom of a well and smeared his shell with bird-lime. The Hare came to bathe his feet and was caught fast, and then his hands and face were caught too. All the other animals came up and beat him for deceiving them and stealing their goods.

Tug of War

One of the most popular of the Hare stories tells how by his cunning he deceived larger but more stupid animals. It is sometimes told about the Tortoise, and in America it is Brer Tarrypin who challenges the Bear, and since he can find no animal of equal size, he ties the other end of the rope to a tree.

In a West African version the Hare was improvident and always borrowed from his neighbours. He had taken so much from the Elephant and the Hippopotamus (the crocodile in some versions) that both got very angry. But the Hare managed to calm them down by promising to give them all and more than he owed, with interest. He went away and made himself a rope of liana from the forest trees, then taking one end to the Elephant the Hare told him that he had only to pull it and he would find a great treasure chest on the end. Quickly he took the other end to the Hippo in the river and told him the same. The two animals took the strain, the Hare running backwards and forwards to cheer them on. As the Hippo was in the river and the Elephant in the trees, and both are short-sighted, this went on for a long time. But finally the Elephant got thirsty and went to the river for a drink, and the Hippo came out of the water, and they recognized each other, while the Hare ran off in safety.

In other versions it is a plain trial of strength, to which the Hare challenged the Rhinoceros and the Hippotamus in turn. They ridiculed the idea that he was stronger than they were, but they pulled against each other from opposite sides of a bush-covered island until the rope

An umbrella top in carved wood from Ashanti, Ghana, which illustrates the proverb: 'The snake lies on the ground, but God has given him the hornbill bird'.

When they had died down he came out, rolled in the black ash, and went to find the Lion. 'See, I am not hurt, look at this ash,' he said. The Lion was astonished and asked if he could have some of the Hare's magical medicine. So the Hare gave him some leaves, looked round for another ant-hill with plenty of grass on it, and told the Lion to lie down there. Then he set fire to the grass all round. When the fire got near him the Lion cried out in alarm, but the Hare told him not to cry – that would spoil the power of the medicine. Then the fire reached the Lion, it singed his hair, burnt his body, set fire to him all over, and he died. So the Hare ran off and told the other animals that he was now their King.

Other fables tell more of Hare's victories over lions, how he broke all the lion's teeth, ate his children, wore a lion's skin, killed many lions, and caused the chief Lion to be stung to death by bees. Another tale from Zambia says that one day the Hare found the Lions eating meat, and he asked if he could stay with them and simply pick the fleas out of their tails. Of course he was deceiving them as usual, and instead of picking out fleas he was digging holes underneath them. As the lazy animals lay stretched out gorged with their meal, the Hare buried their tails in the holes and rammed them down with soil. Then he went home, fetched out a big drum, and began to beat it. The Lions thought that men were coming and jumped up suddenly to run away, breaking off their tails which were fixed in the holes. Then the Hare enjoyed the rest of the meat which they had left.

Hare and Tortoise

This story of the famous race is known in many versions in Africa, sometimes it is the Hare who races the Tortoise, sometimes the Elephant or some other animal. One day the Hare was boasting as usual, and the Tortoise said that he could jump farther than the Hare. The Hare laughed at the very idea, so the Tortoise challenged him to a trial and it was agreed for the next day. The Tortoise hurried off, found his wife, put her in the bushes near the spot that had been decided. When the Hare arrived early next day he found that the Tortoise was waiting for him. He asked the Hare to jump in a certain direction, and the lively beast took a great leap. Then the Tortoise called out that he was coming, slipped into the grass, and his wife appeared in the distance, far ahead of the Hare. The Hare was amazed and said he had not seen the jump, but the Tortoise said that was because his eyes had not been quick enough.

So the Hare acknowledged defeat, but challenged the Tortoise to a foot race which he knew he could win. The Tortoise agreed, but said he was too tired that day and it would have to be the next morning. Then he went home and collected all his family, and spent the night placing them along the road and telling them what to do. Next morning the Hare and the Tortoise started off together and the Hare was soon far ahead. He called back, 'Tortoise', and to his surprise heard a voice ahead saying, 'I am here'. The same happened all along the road, and since it was circular when the Hare arrived panting he found the original Tortoise calmly sitting waiting for him.

Other versions of a race between a slow and fast animal appear in the stories of the messengers of life and death (see pages 54-6), where the slow Chameleon, or another animal, arrives before the fast Dog,

Right: bronze leopard from Benin. A fable says that the Leopard was friendly with the Fire and went to see it every day. But the Fire never returned the visit and the Leopard's wife mocked at this poor friendship. So the Leopard pressed the Fire to visit him, and at last the Fire agreed to come if a path was made for him of dry leaves. He came roaring along, and though the Leopard and his wife escaped their bodies have been marked with black spots ever since. Museum für Völkerkunde, Munich.

but with a less happy message. There are stories of the Tortoise and Baboon, Lizard and Leopard, in all of which he scores off his opponents. Other animals, birds, snakes and other reptiles figure in countless stories. But the cycles of fables about the Hare and the Spider are the most popular.

Anansi and the Corn Cob

In West Africa, where the Spider is called Anansi, the Annancy of America, he is the cleverest of animals and often appears in a mythology where he is the chief official of God though at first he has no name. One day Anansi asked God for one corn cob, a stick of maize grains, promising to bring him a hundred slaves in exchange for it. God laughed but gave him the cob. Anansi set off from heaven to earth and stopped at the first village, requesting a night's lodging from the chief. Before he went to bed he asked the chief where he could put the corn cob safely, explaining that it belonged to God and must not be lost. The chief showed him a hiding place in the roof, and they all went to sleep. But in the night Anansi got up and gave all the corn from the cob to the fowls. When he demanded his cob next morning it had gone, and he made such a fuss that the chief gave him a whole basket of corn to pacify him.

Anansi continued his journey and after a time sat down by the roadside, since the basket was too heavy to carry far. Along came a man with a chicken in his hand and Anansi easily persuaded him to exchange it for all the corn. When he reached the next village the chief put him up, and Anansi asked where the fowl could be hidden, since it belonged to God and must be kept safe. The bird was put in a quiet fowl-house and everybody went to sleep. But Anansi got up, killed the fowl, and daubed its blood and feathers on the chief's door. At dawn he made a great cry, shouting that the bird was gone and he would lose his place as God's captain. Everybody started looking and Anansi suddenly pointed to the blood and feathers on the chief's door. The chief and all his people begged Anansi to forgive them, and gave him ten sheep to calm his anger.

Anansi went off and rested on the way to graze the sheep. Along came some people carrying a corpse, and when Anansi asked whose it was they replied that it was the body of a young man who had died far from home and they were taking him back to the family. Anansi said he was going that way, and offered to take the body if they would take his sheep. They were glad to agree and Anansi went on with the body to the next village. There he asked the chief for rest and explained that he had with him the favourite son of God, who was asleep and needed a hut to rest in. The chief prepared his best room for God's son, and after feasting and dancing they all went to bed.

In the morning Anansi asked some of the chief's children to wake God's son, saying that they might have to shake and even beat him, for he slept heavily. When they came and said they could not wake him, Anansi told them to flog him harder. Still the boy did not wake up, and at last Anansi uncovered the body and cried out that he was dead. He said that the sons of the chief had killed the favourite child of God with their rough beating. There was great wailing among the people, and they were terrified to think of the anger of God. The boy was buried that day, on Anansi's advice, and he said he would try to think of a plan to appease the divine anger. At night he called the chief and said he would have to report the matter back to God. But the chief must give him a hundred young men, to witness that they and not Anansi were responsible for the boy's death. The chief and people gladly agreed, and Anansi set off and finally arrived back in heaven with the youths. He told God how from one corn cob he had gained a hundred fine young slaves, as he had promised.

God was so pleased that he confirmed him as chief of all his host, and gave him the special name of Anansi which he still bears.

How Anansi tricked God

Anansi, the spider, was very conceited and this was often his undoing. When he had been made captain of the divine hosts he began to boast that he was even more clever than God himself. God heard this and was angry. He sent for Anansi and asked him to bring him 'something'. He would not say what it was and Anansi puzzled all day without success, to find out the mysterious object that was needed. In the evening God laughed at him, saying that he had boasted that he was as clever as himself, so he must prove it and find the 'something' without any further help.

Anansi left the sky to look for this 'something' on earth, and after a time he had an idea. He called all the birds to him and borrowed a feather from each of them. He made the feathers into a splendid cloak, flew back to heaven, and perched in a tree against God's house. When God came out he saw the brilliant bird and called all the people together to find out the name of the bird. Nobody could tell him, not even the elephant who knows all the beasts of the forest. Somebody said that Anansi might know, but God explained that he had sent him away on an errand. All the people asked what the errand was and God said that Anansi had boasted that he was as wise as God so he had been sent to get 'something'. The people asked what the 'something' was and God told them that it was the sun, moon, and darkness.

Anansi in the tree heard this, and when God and the people had gone he came down from the tree, threw away his fine feathers, and went off to look for the sun, moon and darkness. It is said that the python was the only one who knew where they were and he gave them to him. Anansi put them in a bag and went back to God. God asked if he had brought 'something', and Anansi said, 'yes', and brought Darkness out of his bag. Then he drew out the Moon, and people could see a little. Finally he took out the Sun, which was so brilliant that some of the people were blinded, and others could see only a little. So it was that blindness came into the world. But others had their eyes shut and the Sun did them no harm.

Anansi and the Chameleon

Anansi and the Chameleon lived in the same village. Anansi was rich, with plenty of children and a large farm, while the Chameleon was poor and alone, and had only a small field to cultivate. But one year the rain fell on the Chameleon's field and not at all on Anansi's farm. Anansi was envious and asked the Chameleon to sell him his field, and when he refused he threatened revenge. Chameleons walk with curious steps over grass and bushes and do not make roads like other people, so there was no path to the Chameleon's field. Anansi therefore got his children to make a wide roadway from his house to the Chameleon's field during the night. In the morning he went there and started pulling up the crops. The Chameleon came and protested and was told to go away – the field

The elephant, one of the most familiar animals of the African scene, inevitably appears in some of the animal fables. This rock engraving from Tassili affirms that he has been familiar to the African people since prehistoric times, and that his distribution was formerly much more widespread than it is today.

137

Animals are the source of many African tales, and they also feature in religious rites. This wood carving of a ram's head comes from the Owo of Nigeria and was placed on a family altar to represent an ancestor. The ram is sacred to Shango, the storm god of the Yoruba, and thunder is believed to be his bellowing.

belonged to Anansi. The Chameleon made a complaint at the chief's court and Anansi was called to account for his action. When both animals claimed the field, the chief asked for proofs. Anansi demanded that they agree it was true that he always made a path while the Chameleon made none, and the latter agreed. The chief sent his servants to see if this was true, and when they reported back he awarded the field to Anansi.

The Chameleon had to go home without field or food, and shut himself up in his house plotting revenge. He decided to dig a great hole, deeper than anyone had seen before, covering it with a roof and leaving just a small hole. Then he set to work to catch hundreds of large buzz flies, which he tied to dried vines and made into a large cloak. When the chief next called his people together the Chameleon went along, walking slowly and proudly in his strange brilliant costume, with the flies buzzing and shining in the sun. The chief himself wanted to buy the cloak but the Chameleon refused. But when Anansi heard of it he promised the chief he would buy it for him, since he was rich. He went to the Chameleon and asked the price. At first the Chameleon refused, but later he relented, saying he was so hungry that if Anansi would give him the food he needed he could have the cloak. He did not want much food, just enough to fill the little hole of his store.

Anansi looked at the tiny opening and promised to sent his children with enough food to fill it twice over. So Anansi's children came with loads of food next day and poured the grain into the hole, but the more they brought the less the hole was filled. For days and weeks they brought food, while the Chameleon stood by and reminded Anansi that he had promised to fill the hole twice over. Anansi was vexed, and kept his children at work till his granaries were empty. Still the hole was not filled, and to keep his word Anansi sold his sheep and cows, and all he had to buy grain to fill the hole. At last the Chameleon declared he was not a hard man, and though the hole was still not full, he would let Anansi off the rest of the debt. He took the cloak out of a box and gave it to him. But during the long time that the cloak had been put away the vines had rotted, and when Anansi took the cloak outside the wind blew it about and all the flies flew away, leaving Anansi with a few withered vines and no crops or money. All the people laughed at him, and since that time Anansi hides in the corners of houses and no longer goes out proudly in the streets as before.

How Anansi became a Spider

Another fable has explains why Anansi become so small. He was once a man, and there was a king who had a magnificent ram, larger than any other, and he forbade anybody to touch it, no matter what it did or ate, under pain of death. Anansi had a large farm and a fine crop of corn was growing there. But one day when Anansi went to look at his corn he was horrified to find that part of the field had been trampled down and the young corn shoots eaten. In the middle of the field, and still munching, was the king's ram. Anansi was so angry that he threw a stone at the ram and killed it. Then he was afraid, for he knew the king's orders.

As he stood under a tree wondering what to do a nut fell on his head, and he picked it up and ate it. Then another nut fell, and he had an idea, like Newton with the apple. He picked up the ram and climbed up with it into the tree, hanging it on one of the branches. Then he went to call on a friend, who was a large spider. He showed him a nut and promised to show him where he could find others. They went back to the tree and Anansi told the spider to shake it, and the dead ram fell down also. Anansi exclaimed that the spider had killed the king's ram, and the spider asked what he should do. Anansi said the best thing was to confess his crime and hope that the king would be in a good mood.

The spider picked up the dead ram and set off. But on the way he stopped to tell his wife what had happened, in case he did not see her again. Anansi stayed outside while the spider went in to speak to his wife. She said her husband was stupid. Had he ever seen a ram climb trees? There must be some trick, so the spider must go on alone to the king, return without seeing him, but report to Anansi that all was well. The spider did this, and when he came back he told Anansi that not only the king was not angry, but he had actually given him some of the meat of the ram to eat. Anansi cried that this was not fair. He himself had killed the ram and ought to have a share of its flesh. Then the spider and his wife seized Anansi and took him to the king. Anansi fell to the ground and begged for mercy, but the king was furious and kicked him so hard that he broke into a thousand pieces. That is why Anansi is much smaller now, and is found in every corner of the house, like a spider broken into many pieces.

African Story

These animal fables are genuine African story, though many of them have travelled far away, to America and Europe. African mythology has not only exported but also imported tales from other parts of the world. Some of the very old stories, though they cannot be dated, may have entered the tropical regions of Africa with negro migrants from the north thousands of years ago. Others came later, with the traders. Some clearly arrived from the Moslem world and there are versions of stories from the Arabian Nights, particularly down the coast of East Africa. A few stories can be traced across to India, to such great collections as the Hindu *Pancha-tantra* or the Buddhist *Jataka* tales. Other yarns came from Europe. Portuguese narratives are found particularly in Angola and Mozambique, and English and French influences are clear elsewhere. Grimm's Fairy Tales are told in many African schools today, so the ancient mythology of Europe enters the African world. In modern times fresh details appear in many stories, such as taking letters up to heaven where the older versions would simply say that messages were sent.

But there is still a great mass of African mythology untouched by any foreign influence, and it is to be hoped that as many myths as possible will be recorded, before they change too much. For they reveal African views of the world, of God and man, of human behaviour and hopes, that are still of great power in the lives of African people in the modern world.

Wooden crocodile from the Congo. In a well known fable the Hare challenged the Elephant and the Hippopotamus or Crocodile to a trial of strength, or promised them hidden treasure to repay his debts. The Hare gave one end of a rope to the Elephant, who was among the trees, and the other end to the Crocodile who was hidden by water. They pulled away till they were tired and gave up, while the Hare made his escape.

Further Reading List

Abrahamsson, H. *The Origin of Death*. Kegan Paul, London, 1952

Arnott, K. *African Myths and Legends Retold*. Oxford Univ. Press, 1962

Cardinall, A. W. *Tales told in Togoland*. Oxford Univ. Press, 1931

Forde, D. (Ed.) *African Worlds*. Oxford Univ. Press, 1954

Fuja, A. *Fourteen Hundred Cowries*. Oxford Univ. Press, 1962

Grianle, M. *Conversations with Ogotemmêli*. Oxford Univ. Press, 1956

Herskovits, M. J. *Dahomey*. Augustin Co., New York, 1938

Idowu, E. B. *Olodumare, God in Yoruba Belief*. Longmans, London, 1962

Itayemi, P. & Gurrey, P. *Folk Tales and Fables*. Penguin African Series, Harmondsworth, 1953

Kenyatta, Jomo. *Facing Mount Kenya*. Secker & Warburg, London, 1953

Krige, E. J. & D. D. *The Realm of a Rain-Queen*. Oxford Univ. Press, 1943

Kuper, H. *An African Aristocracy. Rank among the Swazi*. Oxford Univ. Press, 1947

Lienhardt, G. *Divinity and Experience. The Religion of the Dinka*. Oxford Univ. Press, 1961.

Little, K. L. *The Mende of Sierra Leone*. Routledge & Kegan Paul, London, 1951

Parrinder, E. G. *West African Religions*. Epworth Press, London, 1949

African Traditional Religion. S.P.C.K. London, 1962

Witchcraft, European and African. Faber & Faber, London, 1963

Rattray, R. S. *Ashanti*. Oxford Univ. Press, 1923

Religion and Art in Ashanti. Oxford Univ. Press, 1927

Rouch, J. *La Religion et la Magie Songhay*. Presses Univ. Paris, 1960

Schapera, I. *The Khoisan Peoples of South Africa* Routledge & Kegan Paul, London, 1930

Schebesta, P. *Les Pygmées du Congo Belge*. Duculot, Brussels, 1952

Smith, E. W. and Dale, A. M. *The Ila-speaking Peoples of Northern Rhodesia*. Macmillan & Co., London, 1920

Smith, E. W. and Parrinder, E. G. (Eds.) *African Ideas of God*. 3rd Ed. Edinburgh House Press, London, 1967

Tempels, P. *Bantu Philosophy*. Présence Africaine, Paris, 1959

Verger, P. *Dieux d'Afrique*. Institut Français, Daker, 1954

Wagner, G. *The Bantu of North Kavirondo*. Oxford Univ. Press, 1949

Werner, A. *Myths and Legends of the Bantu*. Harrap, London, 1933.

Acknowledgments

For permission to reproduce the line drawings from Griaule, M: *Conversations with Ogotemmêli* (O.U.P. 1956) which appear on pages 16, 68 top and bottom and 76, the publishers gratefully acknowledge the International African Institute. The publishers also acknowledge the following sources for permission to reproduce the illustrations indicated:

Colour British Museum: Frontis., 121. W. Bruggmann-Holle Verlag, Baden Baden: 49, 52, 73, 80. Giraudon: 129. Michael Holford: 32, 33, 53, 57, 60, 81, 100, 104, 108, 125, back cover. M. L. Lancaster: 84. Musée de l'Homme: 25, 36. Mrs Webster Plass: 101. Vienna, Museum für Völkerkunde: 124. Z.F.A.: 85, 97.

Black and White Paul Almasy: 55 bott., 138. Berlin, Museum für Völkerkunde: 56. Corry Bevington, Arts Council: 34, 64, 71, 127. British Museum: 15, 38 bott., 42, 44 left, 50 bott., 54, 58, 90 bott., 91, 107, 113, 117, 131, 133, 139. Brooklyn Museum: 111 bott. Chicago, Art Inst.: 72, 92. R. B. Fleming: 75. Forman Bros.: half-title, 24. Fed. of Nigeria, M.O.I.: 112. Glasgow Museum: 119, 130. André Held: 63, 93, 132. Michael Holford: 12, 14, 18, 21, 29, 42 top, 66, 67, 70 bott., 74, 88, 89, 90 top, 94, 95, 103, 135. Larousse: 13, 78, 102. Leiden, Museum voor Volkenkunde: 79. Mansell.

111 top. Musée de l'Homme: 11, 20, 27, 28, 31, 38 top, 40, 43, 46, 48, 51, 55 top, 65, 68 left, 69, 87, 96, 98 bott., 99, 118, 137. New York, Museum of Prim. Art: 35, 41, 44 right, 47, 50 left, 62. Geoffrey Parrinder: endpapers, 70 top. Philadelphia, University Museum: 22, 23, 39, 61, 77, 86, 123. Pitt Rivers Museum: 19, 110. Paul Popper: 59, 109, 114, 116. Wm. Rockhill Nelson Gallery: 106. Sotheby & Co.: 30, 37, 98 top. Tervuren, Musée Royale d'Afrique Centrale: 45. United Africa Co. Ltd.: 82, 83.

Index

Figures in italics refer to illustrations